PRAISE FOR PAUL FERRINI'S BOOKS

"The most important books I have read. I study them like a bible!"
Elisabeth Kübler-Ross, M.D., author of *On Death and Dying*.

"These words embody tolerance, universality, love and compassion—
hallmarks of all Great Teachings. They turn our attention inward to
our own divine nature, instead of diverting it outward. Paul Ferrini is
a modern-day Kahlil Gibran—poet, mystic, visionary, teller of truth."
Larry Dossey, M.D., author of *Healing Words: The Power of Prayer
and the Practice of Medicine*.

"Paul Ferrini leads us skillfully and courageously beyond shame,
blame and attachment to our wounds into the depths of self-forgive-
ness. His work is a must-read for all people who are ready to take
responsibility for their own healing." John Bradshaw, author of
Family Secrets.

"A breath of fresh air in an often musty and cluttered domain. With
sweetness, clarity, and simplicity we are directed to the truth within.
I read this book whenever my heart directs, which is often."
Pat Rodegast, author of *Emmanuel's Book I, II and III*.

"Paul Ferrini's writing is authentic, delightful and wise. It reconnects
the reader to the Spirit Within, to that place where even our deepest
wounds can be healed." Joan Borysenko, Ph.D., author of *Guilt is the
Teacher, Love is the Answer*.

"I feel that this work comes from a continuous friendship with the
deepest part of the Self. I trust its wisdom." Coleman Barks, poet and
translator.

"Paul Ferrini's wonderful books show a way to walk lightly with joy
on planet earth." Gerald Jampolsky, M.D., author of *Love is Letting
Go of Fear*.

Book Design by Paul Ferrini
and Lisa Carta

Library of Congress Number
2004110702

ISBN # 1-879159-60-0

Heartways Press
9 Phillips Street, Greenfield MA 01301
www.heartwayspress.com

Manufactured in the United States of America

THE LAWS OF
LOVE

*A Guide to Living in Harmony
with Universal Spiritual Truth*

PAUL FERRINI

Table of Contents

Introduction

The Ten Spiritual Laws discussed in this book are designed to help you connect with your spiritual essence and live in harmony and equality with other human beings on the planet. Each law presents an important aspect of the curriculum of life. Your understanding and eventual mastery of each of these laws will enable you to discover your gift and manifest your full potential as a human being.

Mastery will happen naturally as you complete each of these stages in the learning process.

1. Understanding each Law conceptually
2. Undertaking the spiritual practices related to each Law
3. Teaching the Laws and modeling them in your life

This book is the first part of my *Course in Spiritual Mastery*. The sequel to this book entitled *The Power of Love* presents a ten week program of experiential spiritual practices that will help you to internalize the concepts in this book. Ideally, you would begin to do these practices either while you are reading this book or shortly thereafter.

Beyond that, I invite you to step forward if you resonate with this material and find the related practices to be helpful. I will be training teachers, counselors, consultants and community leaders to bring these principles into active manifestation in their communities.

The people of planet Earth are facing extraordinary challenges. Meeting these challenges will require great ethical and moral clarity from our leaders. It will require that we understand and internalize the great universal spiritual principles presented in these pages.

I hope that you find these principles helpful and that you will undertake the related spiritual practices presented in *The Power of Love*. Beyond that, I invite you to join us in this work in any way that you can.

Namaste,

Paul Ferrini

The Spiritual Law of Oneness

"Love the Lord God with all your mind and all your heart,
for you are of God and from God."

The Spiritual law of Oneness states that anything that comes from God is of God. Anything that comes from the whole is of the whole. Just as God cannot be divided, no expression of God can be divided. Each is whole and complete. There is nothing lacking in any expression of God and all expressions of God are Good. This is the Law that gave birth to the creation of Adam, the first human. That is what it means in Genesis when it says that God made man "in his own image."

Adam is number 1. He is the first. Yet he is also the archetype for the creation of all human beings. Just like Adam, every human being has a son or daughter relationship to God. Every human being is of God and from God.

We call this relationship to our Source "Singularity." In the Kabala this is called the divine spark or essence. It lives in every one of God's creations. It inheres in every heart. It is the divine essence.

When Adam was created, something of God was expressed. That is why we call Adam a Son of God. Jesus claimed the same relationship with God.

But he was not claiming a special relationship. He was claiming the archetypal relationship that all sons and daughters have with their Creator. There is nothing special about being a son or a daughter of God.

Be Ye as Little Children: The Experience of God

God, the Creative Essence of All That Is, cannot be adequately described.

Yet even though we cannot adequately describe God using words and concepts, we can experience God. That experience is essentially MYSTICAL. That is the experience the prophets had. They experienced their oneness with God.

They came to God with awe and respect, but not with fear. After all, they weren't really approaching "an other," but their source, their creator.

In the same way you come to God as a son or a daughter comes to a Father or Mother. You come with an open heart and mind seeking counsel, wisdom, guidance, understanding and support.

There is an intimacy here in the child—parent connection. It is a relationship of love, trust, and respect. This comes naturally to the child, because the child accepts the essential good will of the parent. As a result, the parent is an authority figure for the child. But that authority is conveyed spontaneously and joyfully. There is nothing here of "coercion" or "duty." The child follows wherever the parent leads because the parent knows things the child does not know and the child is in the process of learning these things.

When Jesus told us that we needed to "be as little children" in our relationship with God this is what he was talking about. We need to trust God and follow His direction.

The Kingdom of God is Within

Jesus told us that the kingdom of Heaven lies within. Yet many of us have undertaken a futile search to find God outside of ourselves. That search frequently takes us into the arms of human authority figures who pretend to know something that we don't. When we realize they are just fallible humans like we are, we are pretty disappointed.

After enough religious authority figures and their dogmas disappoint us, we finally get the message that no one else has the answer for us. So we begin to look within for spiritual truth and guidance.

We learn to come to God empty handed, to come to the altar with humility and respect. We learn to speak directly with God from our hearts and to ask Him for guidance or help. That is what real prayer is all about. It is essentially heartfelt and sincere.

We can pray to understand, to accept, and to align ourselves with truth. Our prayers may not be answered right away, but at least we know that we are in the only place where an answer, if there is one, could be.

When you come to God in this way, you enter the inner tabernacle. You open yourself to the possibility of God's love, caring and direction. You open yourself to the possibility that, no matter how much you have struggled or suffered in this life, you can connect with love and truth and bring your life back into harmony and alignment with spiritual law.

There are many outer churches and temples, and you may or may not find them helpful to you. But in a sense, it doesn't matter where you stand on this issue. Whether you have religion or have rejected it is not important here. What is important is that you turn to God within your own heart and mind. If you do that, you can open to God's love for you and accept the authority of His spiritual laws in your life.

To do that is to claim your direct relationship with God as Jesus and all the prophets did. It is to say "I and the Father are One" or I am "from God and of God." It is to accept the fact that you are as much a son or a daughter of God as Adam was.

The Inner Temple

The spiritual law of oneness says that the essence of you lives in God. It is "the way, the truth, and the life" you must align with and follow.

No one else can give you the answers or bring you to that truth. You must come to it voluntarily. You must claim your connection with the creative essence within.

The place where you make this claim is the real temple. It is not an outer place. It is not a place in the world. It is a place in your heart and your mind. It is a holy place, because it is where you meet with God.

No other place in the world is as holy as this one, for in this place alone can you find sanctuary.

Inner Authority

When you find God within your own heart and mind, you will not give your power away to others nor will you seek to become an authority for anyone else. You will reject external authority and discover the authority within.

The authority of all religious institutions and all of the managers and administrators who carry out their policies is essentially artificial and false. The only true authority is the one that Jesus accepted. And that is the authority of God, which can be known only in each person's heart.

Organizations exist in the world and operate according to worldly laws. In that sense, even religious organizations are secular. Therefore they cannot claim any higher or spiritual authority.

There is only one true spiritual authority and it is not an authority that any human being can have over another. Authority that is imposed on one human being by another is essentially a secular authority and is spiritually false.

The only spiritual authority is that of the Creator when it is voluntarily accepted by the son or the daughter. Jesus knew this. That is why he did not want to become an authority for us. Those who made Jesus into an authority figure did not understand this essential truth about Judaism as it was taught by its greatest teacher.

When Jesus said "I and the Father are One" he didn't mean that he was the only one who was one with the Father. He was describing the spiritual connection we all have with our Creator.

Jesus never claimed to be the only son of God. That was the invention of others who didn't have the slightest idea what Jesus was talking about.

Which Authority Do We Accept?

There are two types of authority: Inner Authority and Outer Authority

The first is Spiritual in Nature. It is the divine authority that lives in our hearts and to which we surrender or submit in order to give birth to our spiritual potential.

The second is Worldly in Nature. It is the authority of the secular laws of the world that we live in. We submit to these laws in order to live in an orderly and peaceful way with other human beings.

Both are important. And Jesus told us "Give unto Caesar what belongs to Caesar and Unto God what belongs to God."

The important thing here is that "Spiritual or Inner Authority" never comes from other men and women, not even from Jesus, Moses, Muhammad, Buddha, or Krishna.

Not a single one of us is asked to accept what any other human being says is true (no matter what authority he or she claims). Rather, we are each asked to find our own truth directly through our relationship with God. This relationship is holy and must be respected.

Just as I have a right to a hallowed relationship to the divine and to act in concert with my inner authority, so does every other human being. I must support that right in others if I want to keep it for myself.

Nurturing the Spark

Since God is whole and complete and we are from God and of God, we are whole and complete also. The essence of God is in you and in me, for we are seedlings from the same tree.

The divine spark lives in your heart and mine. We may forget that it is there. We may get lost in the drama of the world and our busy lives. But the spark remains in the core of our being and we can locate it and nurture it.

Indeed, this is what spiritual practice entails. It is our communion with God in the silence of our hearts. It nurtures the divine spark within and helps it to grow into a steady flame that sheds its light on all the dark places of our soul. It illumines error and burns away untruth. It centers us and keeps us connected to our Source so that we can be in the world with compassion for ourselves and others.

This is how we give birth to our divinity while in a human form.

Unity Consciousness

Unity Consciousness is the state of consciousness that we enter into when we feel the presence of God within our hearts and minds. In this state of consciousness, the Spirit of God dwells within us. We may experience this as warmth or energy in our heart center and as peace and tranquility in our minds. We live in the full depth of the present moment without any desire to think about the past or the future. In this moment, we know that we are completely acceptable as we are and so is everyone else. We do not see any problems. There is nothing that we need to change or fix. There is no lack or insufficiency. Everything is perfect as it is. Just as God looked at his creation at the end of the sixth day and said "it is Good," so we look at our lives and know that everything is "good" and acceptable just the way it is.

The reason the Sabbath is important is that it sets aside a regular time each week when we can forget about the struggles of living in the world and remember our connection with God. The Sabbath is an invitation to enter Unity Consciousness and to commune with God. If we do not do this at least once per week, we tend to forget that God is but a hair and a breath away from us. We lose our sense of connection with our Creator. His presence—His light and His love—seem to leave our minds and our hearts.

The earnest spiritual student will begin by making the Sabbath the holy day it was meant to be. But he or she will not be satisfied with that. Weekly remembrance of God is the bare minimum spiritual commitment. The student who wishes to realize his connection with God will make the observance of the Sabbath a daily ritual. He or she will find a time each day for God-communion.

What is our time in communion with God like? It is an experience of bliss for we feel gratitude for all of life and we are blessing and loving all of it.

In unity consciousness, we do not feel separate from God or from any of our brothers and sisters. This is what it means when we say there is "heaven" on earth, for God is present in our hearts and minds.

Jesus lived in a state of Unity Consciousness most of the time. Anyone who experiences her oneness with God moment to moment every day can be said to have attained Christ Consciousness. For Christ means "a human being who is joined with God." The light of God shines in her eyes and the love of God emanates from her heart. Everybody who comes into her presence can see it and feel it.

The Message of Jesus

All the prophets experienced Unity Consciousness. They all communed with God and received guidance from Him in the silence of their hearts.

Their followers, however, had a hard time even showing up on the Sabbath and keeping the ten commandments. To the extent that they obeyed the law, they did so more out of fear than out of love.

By the time Jesus came on the scene, Judaism was as corrupt as it was in Moses' time. Jesus came to overthrow the God of retribution and restore the relationship of love and trust between the people and their God. Of course, that meant he had to practically dismantle the Judaism of his time.

Jesus came to demonstrate unity consciousness and to show people that they could experience God directly. Only the direct and intimate experience of God could motivate people to keep the rest of the commandments.

Jesus knew that ten commandments were a bit much for us. So he told us to focus on two. The first one was "Love the Lord God with all your heart and mind." That is the spiritual practice associated with the Spiritual Law of Oneness.

The second commandments was "Love your neighbor as yourself." That is the practice associated with The Spiritual Law of Equality.

2

The Spiritual Law of Equality

"Every brother or sister is your equal.
Love him or her as you love yourself."

The Second Spiritual Law says that every human being is equal and that you can never love one human being at the expense of another.

Who is equal? Like Adam and Eve, men and women are equal. Black people and white people and yellow people and red people are equal. Hindu, Christian, Muslim, Jewish, and Buddhist people are equal.

People who are straight and people who are gay are equal, people who are sick and those who are not sick, people who have handicaps and those who don't are all equal.

Jesus went even further. He said Hitler and Mother Teresa are equal. He told us we must learn to love everyone, even the most sadistic criminals.

Jesus said, "as you treat the least of them, that is how you treat me." Taken to its extreme, this is not an easy teaching.

The Doctrine of Equality is an absolute teaching. There are no exceptions to it. Therefore it is the only teaching in the world of duality that has True Spiritual Authority. All great spiritual teachers, including Jesus, taught this doctrine.

Any teaching that is at odds with the Doctrine of Equality is false. This doctrine is a yardstick against which all other spiritual teachings can be measured.

The Doctrine of Equality creates a bridge between human beings that opens the channel to divine love. By loving and accepting each other, people can reawaken their awareness of God's love.

The Doctrine of Specialness and the Teachings of Inequality

In contrast to the Doctrine of Equality is the Doctrine of Specialness and the teachings that proceed from it. This Doctrine of Specialness proposes that some people are more worthy or less worthy than others.

The ancient Jews believed, for example, that they were a chosen people. That belief was a fallacy and the Jewish people have paid dearly for it.

Hitler agreed with them and put six million of them to death. Hitler's idea of an Aryan nation was a teaching of specialness.

Such teachings separate one human being or group of human beings from another, give privileges to one and take freedoms away from another. Such teachings can be used to justify various forms of torture, murder and genocide.

Jesus wanted to overturn the concept of "chosen people" because it was a teaching of specialness. He wanted to open up Judaism to all. Faith, he suggested, was not a result of some accident of birth or some right that went with the bloodline. It was a matter of consciousness, of choices made, of the openness of heart and mind.

Ironically, the first thing that happened after Jesus' death is that his followers tried to make him "special." Stories grew up around him to endow him with powers he did not have and did not need. The power of love was sufficient for Jesus. He did not need be the "only son of God, born of a virgin, who walked on water, raised the dead and was physically resurrected." These stories were used to "deify" Jesus and put him on a pedestal. They placed a distance between Jesus and his followers that never existed during his life.

So Jesus was made into the new God. He was special and so were his followers. Enter the Crusades, the burning of heretics at the stake, and all manner of violence and cruelty performed by the Christian Churches and their henchmen in the name of Jesus.

I am not trying to pick on Christians here. Other religions have done the same with their own doctrines of specialness. So you can see how persistent and pernicious the belief in specialness is. Human beings can't seem to get rid of it.

Let us understand clearly what Jesus taught. He taught the spiritual law of equality. He said there is no difference between a Jew and a Gentile, between a man and a woman, between a black person and a white person, between a gay person and a straight person. All are entitled to the same rights, privileges and protections. All are equally deserving of love and acceptance. That is the teaching of the master.

We must see the perversion of Jesus' teaching for what it is. The teachings of Christ have been misunderstood and abused and turned into the teachings of the Anti-Christ. The Doctrine of Equality has been turned into the Doctrine of Specialness. This has been done not just by ruthless dictators and criminals, but by the leaders and spokespeople of many Christian churches.

So be it. This is not said to stir anyone up against anyone else, but merely to set the record straight.

Human beings have only one choice: to treat each other as equals or as unequals. That is the choice that Adam and Eve had, that Able and Cain had, and that you and I have. It is the choice that the Jews and the Palestinians have. It is the choice that all human beings have throughout all periods of history.

So let us understand this choice clearly. As soon as you make Jesus or Moses, or Buddha or Mohammed more worthy than you and put him on a pedestal, you have invested in the belief in Specialness. The strength of these teachers lies in the fact that they share both our humanness and our divinity. They are like us in every way.

Let's be clear. No one is more spiritual than any one else. Spiritually we are all equals. We all deserve love and we all need to learn to give it and receive it without conditions. There is no hierarchy in the spiritual realm.

Those who create levels and hierarchies are teaching the religion of specialness which is the cause of all misunderstanding and hatred on the planet. Do not contribute to this. It does not serve you.

The higher you raise yourself up and the more you put your brother or sister down, the harder it will be for you to find your own redemption.

Jesus asked us: who will cast the first stone? Let it not be you or I. Let us learn to put our stones down and admit our own fears and prejudices.

Types of Earthly Inequalities

Of course, we know that people are not given the same opportunities and talents. Some people are born into riches. Others are born in poverty. Some people are born with high intelligence. Others are born retarded.

Some people are blessed with great health. Others are sickly. Some have physical strength. Others have physical handicaps.

There seem to be great inequalities on the physical, emotional and intellectual levels among the various humans who inhabit the planet.

And the world is certainly so configured that those who are strong could take advantage of the weak, or those who are rich could take advantage of the poor, or those who are smart could take advantage of those who are slow or stupid.

But the Doctrine of Equality says that the strong and the weak, the rich and the poor, the smart and the stupid, have equal rights. One is no more worthy than the other. This is the primary spiritual teaching for planet earth.

Jesus told us "The meek will inherit the earth." The law of equality will prevail in the end.

The commitment to equality is the basis for spiritually informed social action in the world. Equal rights is and has always been the number one cause for all men and women of conscience throughout human history.

The Doctrine of Equality—the great spiritual teaching of the planet—is found in the Declaration of Independence and the Bill of Rights. These are not just political documents. They are sacred texts because they embody the highest truths.

A person who attempts to live the law of equality is constantly asked to stretch and go beyond his or her comfort zone. S/he is frequently asked to let go of biases and embrace a wider and more generous perspective about other people. S/he is asked to "walk in the moccasins" of her opponent and to understand the perspective of those with whom s/he disagrees.

To be committed to human rights—the demonstration on planet earth of the spiritual principle of equality—one cannot have a narrow mind or a closed heart. The spiritual path of those who are committed to equality presents them with ever challenging opportunities to give up false and limited ideas and embrace a deeper and more inclusive truth. Such a person is committed to love not just those who accept his or her values and beliefs but those who don't. That is the teaching of the master.

Do unto others as you would have them do unto you. That is the Golden rule for all human interactions.

Accepting Differences

The teachings of specialness say that in order to love someone we must agree with them. The teachings of equality say that love cannot be based on agreement, because agreement among human beings is a hit or miss affair. We miss it as often as we hit it.

Agreement is fleeting. It comes and goes. But understanding and acceptance can be cultivated. When they are cultivated, two people or countries or religions who disagree can create a culture of mutual caring and respect. Then if both want peace, they can find their way toward it.

The teachings of Specialness say some are right and some are wrong and those who are right must defeat or overcome those who are wrong. The teachings of equality say that neither side has the whole truth. Therefore each side must be respectfully heard.

The way to peace, according to the teachers of equality, is to respect the perspectives and the beliefs of the person on the other side, even if you disagree with them.

This is true for any two people or groups who are polarized. Polarity or disagreement is not bad in and of itself. As long as both sides stay cognizant of their common and complementary interests, the highlighting of differences can create the conditions for a synthesis that benefits both sides.

The Peace Process

The practice of Acceptance says: *I do not have to agree with your position to accept you. As a gesture of my acceptance, I will*

25

hear what you have to say. I will respect what you say, even if it makes me uncomfortable.

That does not sound like such a radical practice, but I assure you that it is. What we are doing with this practice is creating equality. We are not saying "my idea is better than yours" but "your idea is as important and worthy of being heard as mine is."

This is a revolutionary breakthrough in human interaction. It is a shift from specialness—which fuels conflict and misunderstanding—to equality—which supports peace and understanding.

If we want peace in our hearts and peace in the world, we need to let go of the following needs:

1. The Need to be right (or to make another wrong)
2. The Need to agree

As long as we can live with the possibility that there are rights and wrongs on both sides and each side is inevitably biased about which rights and wrongs it sees, as long as we can disagree, not blindly, but with the understanding that comes from listening deeply to each other, and as long as we can see our disagreements in the context of our common and complementary interests, Peace is possible.

As long as peace is possible it is a present as well as a future reality. In a sense, the potential for peace, supported by the willingness of both sides to dialog and understand each other, is the dynamic context in which peace is born.

Sometimes we think of peace as a passive state. And there may be times of ease and tranquility between people and nations. But peace is also a dynamic process in which disagreements arise and are resolved.

Conflict resolution that is peaceful never benefits one side more than another. It always benefits both sides equally, although others outside the conflict might not understand the equation.

War uses force to insure that one side dominates another. Peace uses dialog to insure that neither side dominates and each takes something it considers valuable from the negotiation table.

None of our Judgments are Accurate or Justified

We all have our scapegoats and enemies. We all have people we exclude from the law of equality. We are willing to accept the equality of all other people or groups, but not of "this one," whatever this one is for us.

Moreover, each of us makes hundreds of judgments about other people every day. We try to justify these judgments in our minds. We believe that we are being objective when we are not. We see others, not as God sees them, with understanding and compassion, but as they appear to us in a given moment. We don't have the spiritual perspective that sees the big picture: the web of interconnections that influence the person we are judging. That is a perspective that comes only from a consciousness that is free of judgment.

So one of the first things we must realize on the spiritual path is that our judgments are neither justified nor accurate. What we perceive is not necessarily true. Whenever we see another human being in a negative light, we are attacking him and ultimately attacking ourselves. Seeing another as bad is upsetting not only to that person; it is upsetting to us.

Every inequality that we perceive is simply an error in perception. If we want to live a life of truth, we must correct our perceptions of inequality before we act on them and create suffering for ourselves and others.

Our consciousness is the result of the thoughts that we think and if we are thinking a lot of negative or untruthful thoughts we are going to be fearful and distressed a lot of the time.

Yet it is not necessary to try to force ourselves to be positive when we are thinking negative thoughts. That just strengthens the negativity by making it bad or wrong. What we need to do is become aware of our negative thinking and remember that none of our judgments are accurate or justified.

We need to catch the judgment without beating or shaming ourselves and simply say "I am aware that I am judging" or "I see that I have closed my heart and that when I am in this state I do not see things accurately or fairly." Awareness in and of itself is correction. You do not have to change anything. You don't have to deny the judgment or push it away. You don't need to make it be bad or sick. You just need to be aware of it and hold it gently.

As we hold our judgments gently, we realize that every single one of them comes from fear. Then we can look directly at our fear and hold it compassionately. When we do that, it eventually falls away.

Fear always dissolves in love's presence. And judgments cannot stand when we are committed to the practice of equality.

The Spiritual Law
of Reflection

"First you see through a glass darkly; and then face to face."

The Third Spiritual Law tells us that every person that we meet reflects back to us something about ourselves. Life on the horizontal plane (outer world) is a mirror of what is going on in consciousness (inner world).

Many of us try to find solutions to our relationship problems by looking at our interpersonal behavior patterns and by trying to change them. This rarely works because it does not come to terms with where the patterns originate.

You can try to make yourself and others think and act in more loving ways. You can even attempt to model the spiritual law of equality in your interaction with others. But you may find this difficult or even impossible to do.

Why is this? Because, if you do not feel like an equal, you are not going to be able to treat another person as an equal, no matter how hard you try.

If you hate yourself and are ashamed of something in your life, you are not going to be able to act in a consistently loving way toward someone else.

Something profound stands in the way of our ability to love and to treat others as equals. What is this?

It is our conflicted relationship with ourselves. There are blocks or obstacles to feeling equal to others in our consciousness. Are we willing to look at these impediments?

Most of us are not. We don't want to see our biases and prejudices or look at our hurt or our anger. We don't want to see why we lie to others or break promises. We don't want to look at our fears and insecurities or check out why we are ambivalent or stressed out. We think relationships should be fun and take our minds off our problems. They shouldn't make us work.

So, instead of committing to our own psychological healing, most of us rush off into relationships with other wounded individuals. The results speak for themselves.

Debunking the Romantic Myth

Surprisingly, we are all taken in by the romantic conceit that someone else will be able to make us happy or complete. Yet how can two people who feel broken or incomplete create wholeness together?

It is not possible.

The biggest misconception that we bring to any intimate relationship is the belief that "it is someone else's responsibility to love me and make me feel better." Of course, you can see where this comes from. We all came into this world seemingly dependent on our parents for love and support. And no parent, however loving, is able to meet all or even most of the needs of his or her children. Indeed, many parents, feeling unloved and unworthy themselves, are incapable of loving or caring for their children.

Most children make bargains with their parents to try to get the love and the approval they need. These bargains involve various forms of conditional love. There may be criticism, rejection and even physical abuse. Later, as adults in relationship with other adults, childhood wounds resurface and play themselves out.

We go out in search of a partner who will give us the love that we did not receive from our parents and ironically end up with a partner who is a parental stand-in and replays all the roles our parents played. Destructive and abusive patterns are repeated so that they get our attention.

Why is that?

Because the role of relationship is not to compensate us for all the love we did not get as kids. It is to show us where we need to bring healing to the wounded child within our hearts and minds. It is to show us the co-dependent patterns that cause our suffering and help us learn to give ourselves the love that we so desperately seek outside of ourselves.

Yet, no matter how much we are beaten up in our romantic encounters, some of us are gluttons for punishment. We convince ourselves that we just got a "rotten apple" and that the "apple of our eye" is still out there waiting for us.

Sadly, until we give up the myth that someone else is going to love us, heal us, or make us feel better, we will keep jumping into one co-dependent relationship after another. Eventually, we may lose hope and conclude that something is wrong with us and that we are unlovable.

Of course, that is not true. It's just that we have to stop looking outside of ourselves for love and acceptance.

Before we can have even a ghost's chance for a decent relationship with another human being, we need to learn how to love and support ourselves.

That means that we have to stop hiding from ourselves. We need to find out who we are. We need to look at our doubts and fears courageously. We need to learn to bring love and acceptance to the wounded little kid within.

Until we have established this existential friendship with self, it is difficult if not impossible to be in a relationship with another. If we don't know how to live with ourselves, how can we expect to know how to live with another person?

Loneliness is something that must be faced. Covering it up and jumping into one relationship after another because we are too scared to be alone only postpones the inevitable.

Yet we need to be realistic too. Most of us aren't going to stay alone until we learn to love ourselves. That would be far too logical and tidy. And that isn't the way life tends to be.

So a lot of the practice of getting to know ourselves has to take place "in relationships." That, of course, is the reason why those relationships exist.

But it is all a set up.

We may get involved with someone to try to escape from our

inner pain and conflict, but it doesn't work. Every relationship we have brings us face to face with whatever pain and disconnection we are carrying around.

Raging hormones and sexual attraction, soul-mate fantasies and all the romantic notions that we have about relationship, are just the bait on the hook. But this bait seems to work pretty well, because there are a lot of us fish getting caught and dropped into crucible of relationship.

The Real Purpose of Relationship

So what is the purpose of relationship? It is not, as some suggest, to meet the soulmate and live happily ever.

It is not a romp in the flowery fields of nuptial bliss designed to help us forget ourselves and all of our problems. The purpose of relationship is to help us become conscious of who we are, to help us learn to face our fears and move through them.

Do you think that you can be in an intimate relationship with someone without getting to meet your wounded child and theirs? If you do, you may be in for a few surprises!

The purpose of relationship is not to love and to be loved, because we don't know how to do either. The purpose is to learn how to love and to learn how to be loved.

And how do we learn? By making mistakes. By trespassing on each other and learning how to say "I'm sorry." By learning to take responsibility instead of blaming another.

Relationship is about discovering who we are by looking into the mirror provided by our partner. Now, that sounds rather lofty and dignified. But when our partner is screaming at us or blaming us for something when we were just trying to be helpful, it doesn't seem so lofty.

One thing I can assure you is that if you are not in touch with your shadow when you go into a relationship, your partner will show it to you quickly enough.

Of course, your shadow is not your real self. But you can't find your real self as long as you are acting like a hurt kid or a victim. So you have to come face to face with your shadow. You have to see the bag of fears, worries, angers, insecurities and lack of worthiness that hold you back.

And you know what? Your partner—I don't care who he or she is—is always uniquely skilled in showing you all your weaknesses.

Of course, a viable relationship brings out your strengths too. It is not just about exposing you in the dead of night with your drawers down. We're not talking about punishment here, but mirroring.

Myth and Reality

We begin a relationship in the "mystery" with hormones raging and hyperboles galore, idealizing the beloved, repressing awareness of differences and exaggerating the areas of similarity. We are drunk on the ambrosia of the Gods as we celebrate the perfection of the relationship.

Five minutes later (if you can believe Britney Spears) we are looking at the beloved with eyes full of rage, unmitigated discomfort and irreconcilable differences. And, even if it's 5 weeks, 5 months or 5 years later, it's only a matter of time before Mr.

or Ms. Perfect falls off the pedestal and hits the ground like that Statue of Saddam Hussein we all saw on TV.

Remember, this is not about them anyway. It is about us. The other person is just the mirror into which we look to see aspects of ourselves we have not yet been willing to face.

When we bit deeply down on the hook of romance, we thought we were catching the beloved. Well, here's the news, brothers and sisters: sooner or later we have to take the beloved off the hook. When romance falls apart, trying to keep the hook in place only makes everyone squirm in great discomfort.

Remember, the hook was there for you, not for him or her. The mirror was your mirror. It is up to the other person whether he or she chooses to learn from the encounter. You can't make the other person learn or take responsibility. You can decide only for yourself what you will do.

When romance falls apart and hormones stop raging, what you have are two human beings who are imperfect and ordinary. Each has lost his artificial, idealized aura. Each has hopes and fears, strengths and weaknesses, knowledge and blind spots, emotional gifts and emotional baggage.

Each has a spiritual adult and a wounded child, a bright side and a shadow side. The question is: can each accept the other as he or she is? Can each find a way to individuate within the context of the relationship and support the other in doing the same? Can they create a safe space where it is okay to tell the truth and confess their fears?

If so, the relationship will be reborn from the ashes of fantasy and romance and become a realistic vehicle for the spiritual growth of both people. If not, it will self-destruct as soon as the promises of romantic love are shattered.

Relationships dangle the promise of specialness, but that promise is itself an illusion. No relationship can give to either person anything he or she doesn't already have. Sharing is possible, but completion through the other is not.

The promise of specialness must be rejected sooner or later. In the end, the best any relationship can offer is equality. But that is no booby prize. That is the pearl of great price.

Taking Responsibility: A Crash Course in Boundaries

Many relationships self-destruct because people get so involved in blame and shame and mutual projection that they can no longer see what belongs to them and what belongs to others. In truth it is very simple, but we have to keep remembering it, because the tendency to project is so strong.

Here is a crash course in boundaries in a single sentence: *My thoughts, feelings, words and actions belong to me and your thoughts, feelings, words and actions belong to you.*

So if I'm angry or sad, who is responsible for my anger or sadness? If I criticize, blame or try to fix, who is responsible for my words? If I feel sorry for myself, pretend to be a victim, or hurt myself intentionally, who is responsible for my behavior? Other people may trigger me, but I am responsible for everything I think, feel, say or do.

Okay. "I know I am responsible, but I don't want to be." That's where most spiritual students are. If they didn't know, they wouldn't be spiritual students. But knowing that you are responsible doesn't necessarily mean that you take responsibility. You have to want to take responsibility and you have to practice taking it.

Otherwise you are going to keep projecting your stuff onto other people. There are so many ways to project it's not funny and we are all very creative in finding new ways. If I don't want to take responsibility for my anger, here are a few ways I can try to give it to you:

1. I scream at you or hit you (I feel attacked so instead of finding out why I attack you back).

2. I pretend not to be angry (deny what I am feeling) and tell you that you are the one who is angry (I attribute my thoughts, feelings, words or actions to you).

3. I confess my anger, but I blame you for "making" me angry. I try to give the responsibility for my anger to you.

There are countless ways to project. Understanding how you project can be very helpful, if you have the courage to look at it. But all forms of projection can be boiled down to one simple message:

"It's not about me. It's about you."

That's the content. I am refusing to look at my stuff and trying to hand it to you. Projection is a mechanism of denial (It's not about me) and externalization or false attribution of responsibility (It's about you.)

"I didn't do that; you did. I didn't say that; you did. I'm not angry; you are." And so it goes. We all know how this works because we all do it.

We all refuse to step up to the plate and own that we made a mistake or said or did something we are not proud of.

Why is that? Because we are afraid if we take responsibility, we will be crucified. We're so tired of being blamed, we certainly aren't going to volunteer to "be wrong." We don't want any more blame and shame. So we try to avoid responsibility. And when we do that our errors do not get corrected.

Needless to say, this motif is very circular. In trying to avoid punishment, we give the blame to others and they respond by giving it right back to us. The cycle of attack and counterattack continues ad infinitum until one brave person says something entirely radical and revolutionary:

He says "Okay. I'm mistaken. I said it was about you because I was afraid of being blamed and shamed and punished. But that's not true.

The truth is: It's not about you. It's about me. It was my fault. I was the one in error."

Do you hear that? That is what Jesus called confession. It means getting in touch with your guilt, owning your error and asking for forgiveness. That's powerful. It's transforming.

Now the other person is off the hook and the amazing thing is that once he realizes that you don't want to blame or shame him anymore, he doesn't feel so threatened by you and so he doesn't come after you with his gun or his spear. He puts his weapon down. And, amazingly, he says: "Thank you for taking responsibility and admitting your mistake. It took a lot of courage to do that and I respect you for it."

That is the shift. That is what your spiritual practice can do.

If you have doubt about this, test it out. This week take

responsibility for everything that you think, feel, say or do. Own everything that happens in your consciousness and experience. Be aware of the times when you try to deny something that is yours and try to give it to someone else. When you hear your-self defensively saying "it's not about me; it's about you" notice it and see if you can turn it around. Say to the other person who is pushing your buttons "I want to make this about you, because I'm scared. But I know it's really about me."

A New Look at Right and Wrong

We all like to be right and hate to be wrong. When we are right, we feel empowered and validated. When we are wrong, we feel deflated or even shamed.

Psychologically being right makes us feel that we are "good." It feeds our ego. And being wrong makes us feel that we are "bad." It feeds our feelings of unworthiness.

Is it any wonder that most of us "want to be right" and don't want to be wrong? This desire is so strong that we often "act like we are right" even when we know we are wrong!

There aren't many rewards for "being wrong" in our world.

Yet Jesus encouraged us to admit our sins. Surely, he did not feel we were "bad" if we made a mistake and owned up to it. In fact, he suggested that the practice could open an important doorway for us.

What happens if we interpret being right and wrong in a new way?

Let's say we take some of the "pride and praise" away from being right. When we are right, our ego is being fed and that doesn't help us make much progress on the spiritual path. So being right is okay, but it's not a spiritual event, especially if we gloat over it.

But when we are wrong, our ego is not being fed. Being wrong gives us an opportunity to be humble: to admit that we did not know something and to be willing to learn. Now that is a spiritual event.

That's what Jesus meant when he invited us to confess our mistakes. It was not an invitation to suck up blame and invite punishment. It was an opportunity to be humble and learn. It was a spiritual event.

Jesus tried to help us realize that being "wrong" was not bad. It was just being human. We all make mistakes. That is just the way it is.

"No," he said. "You are not bad. You are not condemned by your error. Your error simply offers you an opportunity to learn and grow."

But this is "New Testament" thinking, and most of us are still living in "Old Testament" consciousness, waiting for the hammer to drop. Jesus said: "Wait a minute folks. God is not an angry God. He doesn't want to punish you. He just wants to help you learn from your mistakes. And you can't learn if you don't admit your error."

Still none of us ran exuberantly to the halls of confession. We didn't really believe it was okay to make a mistake. We didn't really think God or our brother and sister would forgive us.

So we held onto our error and the guilt attached to it. We did not purge it or confess it. It was heavy on our heart, but we could lift the pain.

Jesus told us "Don't be afraid. Everyone here is just like you. Be courageous and tell the truth. No one will condemn you for your error because by condemning you he would be condemning himself. But by accepting you and your humanness, by forgiving your mistake, he would be creating the conditions for his own redemption."

Jesus asked us to unburden our hearts. He asked us to share our pain with our brother and sister.

He asked us to step up to the plate, acknowledge our errors and ask for forgiveness. You see the shift that he was calling for?

Needing to be right keeps us cut off and isolated from our brothers and sisters. The only way we can reconnect with them is to tell the truth and admit our mistakes.

Remember, sometimes it's wrong to be right. You can really beat someone up with the truth. Self righteous behavior does that. And sometimes it is right to be wrong, because you become humble and willing to learn.

If you want to find out how powerful it is to admit your mistakes, just start doing it. Next time you know you are wrong, admit it. Apologize. Make amends.

If you can't do it in the moment, do it later. If you can't tell the person you offended, tell his mother or his sister. Tell someone.

Confess your errors so that you do not hold onto your guilt and continue to rationalize or justify your mistake. Confess your error so that you don't have to try to cover it up. That can be exhausting and, after hundreds of denials, you might start to dislike yourself a little.

Remember, most sins are unintentional. Don't make them

intentional by holding onto them. Fess up and let them go.

Ask for forgiveness. You might be surprised to see how easy it is for people to forgive you when you are honest and take responsibility for correcting your mistakes. Indeed, you might find that you make more friends than you do denying your guilt.

What do you think? Maybe it's not so terrible to be wrong? Maybe you can be wrong and still be a good person?

I know it's an outrageous idea, but why not give it a shot?

4

The Spiritual Law of Manifestation

"Consciousness is creative.
You are responsible for what you create."

The Manifestation Process

Manifestation is the process by which we take some energy or idea which is not yet in form (unexpressed) and bring it into form (expression). It is another word for creating.

Just as God is creative, we are also creative. And just as God is responsible for creating us, we are responsible for our creations. Learning to create and how to be responsible for our creations is one of the cornerstones of the curriculum in the school of life.

You Can't *Not* Create

All of us are constantly creating, whether we are aware of it or not. Of course that doesn't mean that we are creating what is good for us and for the people we love. We have to learn how to do that.

Every time you think, you are engaged in the creative process. Every time you feel something and act on it, you are in the process of creation. One of the spiritual principles we accept is that "consciousness is creative." The idea and the feeling behind it (our conviction) initiate the manifestation process.

Now that doesn't mean that if you think the word/concept "elephant" with great conviction there will be an elephant sitting in your driveway when you get home from work. But if elephants are important to you and you go to the zoo to see them and you dream about elephants at night, it might not be too long before you take a safari and view the elephants of the Serengeti. Of course, I'm not saying that it is impossible that you will have an elephant sitting in your driveway. I'm just trying to illustrate the fact that the principle "consciousness is creative" is not some kind of magical thinking. It works because we put energy into it.

So the first thing we have to understand about the law of manifestation is that what we really care about and energize most is what is most likely to come into form. If we think casually about something and we feel half-hearted about it, it isn't likely to manifest.

Now, please remember, you can't fake it. If you pretend to be interested in something, it has little creative power. That's why most affirmations don't work. People don't really believe them.

44

That's why they keep saying them over and over again. But until they really believe what they are saying the words don't have much power. On the other hand, if you have a statement that you know in every cell of your body to be true and you say that statement with conviction, the creative power of the words comes across. Others can feel your conviction and they pay more attention to you. Even your own subconscious begins to listen.

Creativity Requires Commitment

Commitment is necessary for anything to manifest. If that commitment exists on all levels—physically, emotionally, mentally and spiritually—then manifestation is practically guaranteed.

When alignment on various levels does not occur, what is created will reflect the ambivalence or conflicts in consciousness.

Not only do you need to believe in the idea and feel excited about it and thus energetically anticipate its outcome, but you also need to do everything within your power on the physical level to facilitate its manifestation.

Sometimes people think "Well, I'll just put the idea out and let God do the rest" and then they get tired sitting around waiting for God to take care of things. Perhaps they get angry at God or think there is something wrong with them (Maybe they aren't spiritual enough to get God's attention, etc).

But what makes them think God cares a flying flake for their idea? And even if God did care, when did God say that He would take responsibility for our creations?

You see, we forgot that we are the ones who volunteered to

eat the apple. We were the ones who wanted to have the ability to create. We just need to learn to use this ability responsibly.

Magical Thinking does not Lead to Creative Manifestation

The universe doesn't serve things up on a silver platter, at least not since the days of the Garden of Eden. We all need to go out and pick the vegetables and learn how to cook them. You have heard the expression "Chop Wood, Carry Water." In the old days it used to be "Shut up and clean the toilets."

A lot of people have some kind of weird idea that someone else is going to do the dirty work. Someone else is going to take care of them. Of course, a lot of these folks were trust fund babies. They were coddled and protected from the struggle of life so they never learned how to create or take responsibility for anything. But, not to worry, even the Buddha was a trust fund baby. So there's hope for all of us.

Just as the Buddha had to crash through the gates that hid all of the struggle and poverty around him, we all have to meet suffering head on.

Getting the silver platter—just in case it might be an option for you—is really no blessing, because it keeps you from learning what you need to learn.

So folks, nobody else is going to do the dirty work. Not God and not your neighbor. You are the one who has to clean the toilets. If you aren't willing to clean the toilets, you aren't going to learn leadership skills, because you can't ask anyone else to do something you are not willing to do.

Pride is dysfunctional on the spiritual path. Humility is required.

Manifestation does not happen if you aren't willing to do whatever needs to be done. But when you are willing, the potential is there to move mountains.

When you role up your sleeves and go to work, others see your example and join with you. Before you know it, all the sandbags have been filled up and the flood waters have been held back.

But try to tell others to pick up their shovels when you are sitting in your air conditioned Mercedes in your three piece business suit and see what happens. You'll be lucky if they don't throw you and your Mercedes into the river.

So the main question to ask when it comes to your creative process is: Are you willing to do whatever needs to be done? Are you committed?

And this is a question you need to ask yourself every day, because you can be sure that your commitment will be tested, again and again. You have to really want something to bring it into manifestation.

Daily Practice as a Demonstration of Commitment

Some people say that they want to become great athletes, but they can't seem to get themselves to the gym every day. Others say they want to be great musicians, but they would rather go out with their friends than stay home and practice. These people will not meet their goals because they aren't willing to practice. No matter how much talent you have, no matter how brilliant your ideas are, you will not manifest your potential if you don't commit to a daily practice. Generally speaking, great writers, great artists, great athletes, great teachers are not born over night. The mastery they demonstrate is a direct result of thousands upon thousands of hours of committed practice.

Remember: great journeys begin with the next step. It doesn't matter how small or how ambitious your goal is, you still have to begin by taking the first few concrete steps. Find a teacher and start practicing. Then find a better teacher and practice harder. Commit every day to what you are doing.

That's the only way you can accomplish your goals and fulfill your dreams.

Magical Thinking? Forget it. Don't waste your time. Not willing to chop wood or carry water? Forget it. Stay on your trust fund or find a spot to sleep under the bridge. Want to jump over that field full of cow dung or avoid the muddy field on the way to the stage? Try it and see what happens.

The universe is unlikely to reward you for being too fearful or too proud to get your hands dirty. And, if it should reward you, better watch out. Gifts that are not earned can be taken away as quickly as they are given.

Self-Confidence

Now you aren't cleaning the toilets to impress God or your spiritual teacher. You are cleaning the toilets because it has to be done and someone has to do it. You are learning to do a good job, to work hard, and to feel a sense of accomplishment. That means a lot more than you think it might.

You are learning to empower yourself. You are giving yourself the message on all levels "I can do it!"

People who are too proud to clean the toilets and hold out for loftier jobs are saying "I won't do it" and it doesn't take long before this translates into the belief "I can't do it." By saying "No" to the opportunities life gives to you to participate, you hold yourself apart from others and miss the chance to build your self-confidence.

The biggest obstacle to the Manifestation Process is: having too grandiose a vision and being unwilling to do the little things that are necessary to take advantage of the opportunities that life provides. On the other hand, the greatest potential for manifestation happens when we choose a modest goal and work hard to accomplish it.

In the first case, we teach ourselves to fail and erode our self-confidence. In the second case, we teach ourselves to succeed and build our confidence in ourselves.

Unless we take small steps that build our self-confidence and show us that "we can do it," we are going to begin to wonder if the universe is friendly and if there is a place for us here. But if we are honest, we have to admit that our failure or lack of accomplishment stems from the fact that we said "No" instead of "Yes" to an opportunity that presented itself. It all comes back to our pride and lack of willingness to do what needed to be done.

The Four Components of the Manifestation Process

The manifestation process has four clear components.

1. We have to have a clear goal, idea or a vision.
2. We have to believe in it and be committed to it.
3. We have to be willing to do whatever needs to be done.
4. We have to let go of our pictures or expectations of the way our goal is going to be met or our idea /vision is going to be realized.

We've already discussed the first three of these components. Without them, there won't be enough energy to bring our idea into manifestation.

However, even if we have the vision and the energy behind it, we can still fail if we are rigid and uncompromising in its implementation.

Every idea that anyone has is going to be shaped, refined and even transformed as it moves into manifestation. As it comes into the world and is shared with others, our vision has to encounter many unanticipated forces and factors. Obstacles—some real and some imagined—will appear and have to be negotiated. Areas of vagary or confusion will need to be thought about, better defined or refined. Assumptions will need to be tested and feedback integrated.

This is all part of the creative process. It does not happen in a vacuum.

Unlike the initial vision, which is internal, nurtured silently, and thus seems both coherent and predictable, the expression of that vision in the world can be quite surprising, dynamic and unpredictable. We may anticipate a big splash and encounter boredom, apathy, or stony silence. Or we might anticipate acceptance and enthusiasm and find out our vision is controversial and pushes people's buttons. This is all par for the course.

Thus, one of the key components of the spiritual law of manifestation is: "Nothing happens the way we think it will happen." That is because we are not the only ones thinking and our ideas are not expressed in a vacuum.

And so one of the psychological adjustments the process requires from us is that we "surrender our concepts of the way we think things should be." The difficulty of doing this should not be underestimated. Most of us feel a certain ownership of our ideas ("It's my baby, not yours") and need to feel that we have control of what happens.

If we insist on having control, our creative process may abort. In other words, to create successfully, we have to let go of our creations. They have a life of their own.

The Nine Stages in the Manifestation Process

The best metaphor for understanding this and other key aspects of the creative process is the parent-child metaphor, because our ideas are our babies and, like our babies, they grow up and need to be given wings.

So let us think of the creative process in nine stages. They are as follows:

1. Conception
2. Gestation
3. Birth
4. Early Childhood
5. Adolescence
6. Adulthood
7. Maturity
8. Death
9. Rebirth

At *conception*, the idea or vision comes to us. It might arise "out of the blue" or it might simply well up in consciousness. It might be sudden like a bolt of lightning, or it might be gradual, like a wave rising up within consciousness. Either way, it is the gift, the moment of conception, the seeding of the new.

At *gestation*, we are pregnant with the idea or vision. We nurture it and allow it to grow silently within. We don't tell others about it until we are so filled with it that everybody knows that we are pregnant. Only then do we start talking about it.

At *birth*, the idea is born in the world. It needs a lot of active care and support. In fact, we are on-call practically 24 hours per day. We have to make sure that our baby is safe, guarding the integrity of the vision and allowing in only those friends and family members who love our baby and are willing to help us take care of it.

In *early childhood*, we start to trust our child with strangers, send him to school, allow him to engage with peers and other adults. Our vision is tested gently in the marketplace and we get feedback from others, refining our vision accordingly so that it can be more effective and compelling in the world.

In *adolescence*, we begin to realize that our baby is growing up and has a will and a life of his own. We need to start letting go, letting our idea be out there in the world on its own terms. We are still supportive, but from a distance.

In *adulthood*, we detach and let go. We know our child has his own life to live and work to do. We are grateful when the child comes home and visits us, but we don't expect much. Hopefully, we are getting on with our own life. Perhaps a new creative project announces itself and needs our attention.

At *maturity*, we know our idea has fulfilled its potential. It has made its contribution to the world. We are grateful, but we know that no idea stays in vogue forever. Ideas come and go. That is natural. So we are willing to let go. After all, it is not our idea any more. We have given the gift. It belongs to others now.

In *death*, our idea recycles. The essence remains and is replanted, perhaps in our own mind or in the minds of others. And the form—which has become worn, torn, or dysfunctional—along with any impurities or distortions that have attached to it—is dissolved in the fire of love and truth.

In *rebirth*, the idea finds a new form of expression that is relevant to the world that it lives in. Truth is eternal. It lives at all times. It merely changes form in order to better meet the needs of the specific time and place.

If we can understand this elegant, organic process in this profound way, we will master the art of living as a parent and as a creative being.

The Importance of Staying Grounded

One of the common challenges for people who are drawn to spiritual teachings is to keep their feet firmly on the ground. Some people read spiritual books, take classes and workshops, and even join religious cults in an attempt to run away from the challenges of daily life. They want to escape the difficulties of learning skills, getting and keeping a job, taking care of themselves and others. They want to deny their human needs and responsibilities and go right to God.

I have met thousands of spiritual students who wanted to buy a ticket on the rocketship to heaven. They not only wanted it soon. They wanted it today. And it did not matter what it cost. If they had money, they would pay the asking price. If they didn't have money, they would sell themselves, their spouses and their children into bondage and slavery.

This motivation "to escape from the world"—to by-pass the levels of emotional healing and mental purification required for enlightenment—inevitably leads to a cul de sac. Those who promise salvation in this way, are no better than the clergy selling Indulgences in Martin Luther's day. You can't buy your way into heaven. And anyone who tells you that you need their special teaching or method to open the pearly gates is probably going to take your money, your dignity, and your freedom. Of course, they cannot do this without your permission.

Wholesome spirituality is not motivated by a desire to escape the challenges of life. It is motivated by a desire to take up those challenges with greater confidence and skill.

More than one smart Swami I know made all of his followers

get a job. And it wasn't always the most glamorous or prestigious job. The point is that spiritual work is every day, every moment. It must be integrated into our lives, no matter where we live and what we are doing.

This is the opposite of the rocketship to heaven. Call it the creaky rickshaw to heaven, if you want. And you are the one pulling the carriage. It is painfully slow. In fact, it takes so long, you begin to wonder if you will ever get there. Indeed, you begin to think that perhaps heaven doesn't exist. And then, just when you are about to give up, the rickshaw turns into a pumpkin, you face your fears as Jesus did in the desert for 40 days and nights, and then you realize that the vehicle was immaterial. It was an illusion. You didn't have to go to heaven, because heaven was already there. You just pulled that heavy cart around out of ignorance.

Of course, when you have been logging thousands of miles on foot, you are so happy to be rid of the cart, you don't even think to be bitter about all the time you wasted and all the muscles you strained. You are just glad to be free.

Yet, if you don't drive that cart to Timbucktoo and back, you won't believe me when I tell you heaven is right here. The journey is necessary not because it brings you to some far-away truth, but because it brings you back to the truth that is staring you in the face. Obviously, you don't see it now, or you would start cheering, just like the rickshaw guy did.

So you see, your difficulty has nothing to do with getting access to the truth. You all have access to it. You don't have to pay any money. You don't need to go on any special pilgrimages or trips. You just need to believe the truth when you see it.

Most people aren't looking for the truth. They're looking for the package it is wrapped in. They have a certain idea of the way it's going to look, the type of messenger who will deliver it (they might even be able to tell you what he is wearing when he rings the doorbell). Someone can show up in their lives and give them the gift of truth without any show or artifice and they won't know what they have been given. Because bells didn't go off, they take the gift home and stash it in the basement or some closet corner.

Yes, it is true that "the truth will set you free." But first you have to recognize the truth. And then you have to commit to it and live it every day.

It's really quite simple. There is nothing esoteric about it. But that, of course, is why everyone overlooks it and goes on searching for "the next big thing."

So let's get real. The more glamorous your spiritual practice is and the loftier the goals, the more likelihood that it is just feeding your ego and lining the pockets of some swami, psychic or spiritual loan shark.

Truth does not have a price. It doesn't have a face. It has no appearance. It is all essence. That's why it's so easy to overlook.

5

The Spiritual Law of Free Will

*"Victims say they have no choice.
Creators know they always have a choice."*

The Spiritual Law of Free Will states that we have the freedom to choose between good and evil or (if you don't like those terms) between what helps and what hurts.

Furthermore, it tells us that choice is a condition of our creation. We are born with the capacity to choose freely and we are constantly exercising it, even if we don't think that we are.

If you do not feel that you are making choices in your life, it may be because you are not doing so consciously. Many of your choices might be being made at an unconscious level.

Unconscious choices are decisions that we make without thinking or consideration. For example, breathing is not usually something that we think about or consciously "choose" to do. We don't tell our lungs to breathe air or our heart to pump blood. These are done by our autonomous nervous system.

To take another example, every time you eat something you are making a choice. You could eat a carrot or a cake, a salad or a steak. If you are a vegetarian you make certain choices. If you are carnivorous, you make other choices. And the choices you make tend to become repetitive and predictable. The meat eater doesn't have to think about whether he wants a steak. He just puts it on the grill, cooks it and eats it.

Repetitive choices are by nature unconscious ones. The way we squeeze the toothpaste tube, the position we sleep in, the shows we watch on TV or the way we walk and talk are all things that we just "do." We don't think about whether or not we are doing them.

Yet every thing we do is a choice. We could stop and ask "Should I drink a cup of coffee in the morning?" or "Is it good for me?" But most coffee drinkers don't ask such questions, just as most smokers don't ask "Should I have this cigarette?

Many choices that we make are repetitive and unconscious. They may even be addictive. Addictive behaviors seem to be the opposite of choice or free will. But the potential of choice remains. The alcoholic can refuse to take the drink. The heroin addict can refuse to put the needle in his arm.

Most do not, because most don't want to think about what they are doing. They don't want to be aware of the fact that they might be hurting themselves or others.

The spectrum of choice runs from conscious choice on one end to addictive or compulsive choices on the other.

1. *Conscious choice* is a choice that we have carefully considered. We have made a decision based on having good information, some of which may and often does come from our personal experience. When we choose consciously, we are clearly exercising our free will.

2. *Repetitive choice* is a choice that we make because we made it before and we are familiar with its results. We could question the validity of this choice and stop making it if we really wanted to. We can become aware of a repetitive pattern and change it. For example, we could stop eating potatoes every night and have a salad instead.

3. *Addictive or compulsive choices* are choices we can't stop making. We can't stop eating or drinking or having promiscuous sex, or smoking or drugging, or letting our spouse beat us up. Or we can't stop washing our hands every five minutes. Such choices often result from dysfunctional phobias or from PTSD suffered during war, imprisonment, rape or in some other abusive situation. At this end of the spectrum, it doesn't feel like we a have a choice. While it is true that we could stop our compulsive or addictive behavior, it is highly unlikely that we will do so.

Our goal as spiritual students is to heal any addictive or compulsive behaviors that we have. For some of us, this is a major piece of healing work that might take years to accomplish. In addition, we want to begin to question our repetitive patterns to see if they are really helpful to us. Gradually, we want to be making as many choices as we can consciously and without any pressure or duress.

Let Freedom Ring: Claiming Our Freedom to Choose

Claiming our freedom to choose requires certain assumptions. The most important of these assumptions is we are not victims. We are creators.

Circumstances may limit victims, but they do not limit creators. Victims feel that they have no choice. Creators know that have a choice and must exercise it.

Creators know that they are free to choose the life they want. Indeed, they know that it is their responsibility to do so. They know that there are no excuses for not choosing.

Creators work with the resources at hand and find a way to achieve their goals or manifest their vision. Victims complain that the resources they need are insufficient or not available.

Creators grow and learn from their mistakes. They give up limiting ideas and adopt ideas that are more flexible and empowering. Victims are discouraged by their mistakes and try to blame others for their failures.

Creators are patient with others and listen to their feedback. Victims think others are against them and resist their input.

Creators refuse to let anyone take their freedom away. Even when the circumstances that surround them are severely limiting, they find a way to stand up for themselves and exercise their freedom to choose (for a profound example see Victor Frankl's *Man's Search for Meaning*). Victims give in, lose their dignity and their will to live.

Creators make the following key assumptions:

1. I am free to decide in any moment.

2. I decide based on my awareness at the time.

3. I may make a mistake and that of itself doesn't shame or condemn me.

4. If I am willing to learn from my mistake, I can correct it and make a better choice next time.

Victims on the other hand love to say "I had no choice. I had to do it" or "the circumstances forced me to do it." They don't acknowledge their errors or take responsibility for correcting them. That's why they remain victims.

Taking Responsibility for our Choices

When you own the choice, it doesn't mean that you need to defend or justify your choice if it turns out to be a bad one. In fact, if you do that, you will just aggravate and reinforce the error. Taking responsibility often means not just "owning the choice" but also "owning the error." When you "own the error" you are saying "I am willing to learn from this experience. Next time I can make a better or more informed choice."

That enables you to take a major step forward in exercising your free will. For free will and learning go hand in hand. One leads naturally to the other.

Without free will we don't learn anything, because we aren't given the opportunity to make mistakes. That is why free will is one of the defining characteristics of the human experience. It suggests that we can grow in skillfulness and understanding.

We can become more aware, more compassionate. We aren't just stuck on some level, limited to the circumstances we find ourselves in. We can move out of the box we have created around us. We can become disentangled from the web of definitions, opinions and beliefs we have assembled within consciousness. We can see their limitation and grow beyond them.

Because of free will, we are teachable. We are redeemable.

Transcending Limiting Beliefs

We all perceive things through our conceptual filters. We see things according to our values and beliefs, our biases and prejudices, and the conclusions we draw from our past experiences. In Corinthians we are told: "First we see through a glass darkly, and then face to face." That means if we want to see things accurately, we have to remove our dark glasses, our conceptual filters.

Of course, it's hard to remove our conceptual filters if we don't know what they are. For example, we might hold a belief that gay people are bad or not as morally correct as straight people. That belief will prevent us from seeing the full humanness of any gay person we meet. It will limit us and distort our perception of reality.

It takes real humility to realize that what we perceive or believe may not be true. Indeed, no matter how spiritual we think we are, there is always some portion of Reality that we don't see accurately. We cultivate humility when we acknowledge our false beliefs and our prejudices and open our minds and our hearts to a greater, more inclusive truth.

Your values and beliefs are your operating assumptions in life. For example if you believe "all people are equal" you will live a different kind of life than you will if you believe "white people are better than black people" or "Christians are better than Jews" or "men are better than women." If you believe "The man must always be taller than the woman for a relationship to work" or "I can only marry a Jewish person" you may discount a person who would otherwise be compatible with you.

Values and beliefs limit the field of possibility. They say "I care about this. I choose to live my life this way. This is what is important to me." They are a way of setting priorities in life.

A young person who is concerned with "prestige" or "reputation" may decide to apply only to the top colleges in the country. If this person is smart enough to get into one of these schools, this operating agenda might not hold him or her back. But if the person can't get into these schools and refuses to apply to others, the operating agenda might be dysfunctional and might need to be revised.

Values and beliefs change as we learn to face the challenges of life. While we can always move backwards and adopt more restrictive values in response to hurts we have suffered, the natural spiritual progression is toward higher, more inclusive values that help us open more deeply to acceptance and love for ourselves and others.

Changing those limiting values and beliefs that no longer support our growth and development as human beings is an important part of the learning process. It is healthy to do so. It helps us to expand our consciousness.

Surrendering the False Self

The False Self is the persona or mask that we wear to gain acceptance and approval from others. It is generally a very limited, one dimensional image of ourselves that does not include the full range of our humanness.

When we live life through our persona or mask, we aren't living authentically. We aren't letting others see our doubts and fears. We're stuffing all that and just showing the veneer: the politically and socially correct surface.

That is tragic, because the False Self cannot experience real intimacy. It can meet others only on the surface of life. There is no depth here, either personally or interpersonally.

So if we want to experience intimacy, we must drop the mask and let people see us as we truly are. That takes great courage.

Choosing to be ourselves is the most important and courageous choice that any of us will make. We should not underestimate the difficulty of making this choice on an ongoing basis in our lives.

Each of us is asked to surrender the False Self not just once, but numerous times. That is because our mask is always changing and becoming more sophisticated.

Every encounter in life offers us the challenge of revealing our whole self—with all of its raggedness, ambivalence, conflict and confusion—or our neatly trimmed and smartly decked out one-dimensional persona. We might be in pain or in conflict, but our persona doesn't show that, unless of course it cracks.

Sometimes, no matter how hard we try to maintain our mask, it splits right down the middle, and then Humpty Dumpty comes tumbling off the wall. While this can be disconcerting to us, it is a positive spiritual event. It gives us the opportunity to bring our real self forward into expression.

When the false self cracks, we are in crisis. We can no longer function the old way and our old way of life starts breaking down. It doesn't work any more. But if we let the mask come off, this so called 'breakdown" of our lives can become a kind of spiritual "breaking through."

Of course, our friends and family may not understand or sympathize with what is happening to us. They may want us to keep our mask and our old social definitions in place. It may be too painful to try to meet their needs and expectations anymore. Instead, we may need to give ourselves permission to get out of that straightjacket.

For many people the explosion of the "box" or the "straightjacket" results in the psychological death of the old familiar person and the rebirth of a new, more authentic person whom friends, family and community members may not recognize. This new person often makes them feel uncomfortable, because he or she no longer confirms and supports the lifestyle and beliefs they have chosen.

People are often threatened by anything that deviates from the status quo, however sick or dysfunctional the status quo may be. And in their fear they may try to ostracize, reject, or marginalize those who are different or unique.

We may talk about authenticity, but when it looks us in the eyes, we aren't so sure we like what we see. Authentic people do not homogenize very easily. They can't be described or understood using labels like Divorced, Babyboomer, Single Mother,

Democrat, Christian, Caucasian, or Southerner. They can't be pigeonholed. They don't fit into any clear demographic. They don't belong to any easily formed or ready made group. Their allegiances are more complex and chaotic.

To put it simply, authentic people are harder to manipulate and they can't be easily controlled.

We may pay lip service to concepts of authenticity with slogans like "Be all you can be." But I don't think the army really wants its recruits to demand to be treated as unique human beings, because that would not be congruent with the Army's authority structure or its code of discipline.

The fifth spiritual law is about having the freedom to be who we are and make the choices that are best for us. It is about defining ourselves and ultimately going beyond our own self definitions. It is not about being defined by others or by their expectations of us.

It is not about living by someone else's values, standards or rules. It is about freedom, not imprisonment. It is about getting out of the box, not about boxing ourselves or anyone else in.

It is about freedom, not capitulation. It's about independence, not conformity.

The fifth spiritual law is about valuing and honoring our own experience, not about accepting the experience of others as a blueprint for us. We have our own blueprint.

6

The Spiritual Law of Compassion

"Your good and that of your brother and sister
is one and the same."

The spiritual law of compassion tells us that all human beings are worthy of love and acceptance. It tells us that our common needs, common aspirations and common experiences far outweigh our individual differences. Although our differences need to be honored and respected, it is our similarities that allow us to gather together and support each other in our human journey.

Cooperation among people is the fruit of the law of compassion in operation. People cooperate because they feel connected to each other as brothers and sisters and because they have common or complementary needs.

Selfless service to others, volunteer and philanthropic work, as well as efforts for peace, human rights and social justice arise from the law of compassion in operation.

The Family as a Metaphor for Support and Acceptance

The family is the first unit of social connection or disconnection we experience as humans. Our family is the place where we feel that we belong or that we don't belong. It is where we feel loved and accepted or where we feel criticized and rejected.

Families are places where we experience our innocence or learn to feel shame. Most of us experience a little bit of each.

A positive self image and sense of self worth result from belonging to a successful family unit. Of course, no family is perfect. But when our family experiences are mostly positive, we enter adulthood feeling loved, accepted, cared for, valued, and supported. On the other hand, when our family experiences are primarily negative, we enter the adult world feeling unworthy and disconnected from others.

Acceptance from our family helps us learn to trust those around us. Rejection from our family makes us feel suspicious and distrusting of others.

Whatever our family experience is, we must learn to accept it and work with it. Feeling victimized by it will not empower us to create a positive environment of acceptance and love in our lives.

Those whose family experience is abusive or traumatic in some way often leave home wounded and angry. They need to come to terms with their hurts and make time for emotional healing.

If they don't, they will go through life attempting to make everyone else pay for their wounds.

Some people seek to meet their needs for belonging, approval or support by joining religious groups, cults, gangs, social clubs, or secret societies. Often they pay a high price to belong and may have trouble breaking free from the group. They give their power away and don't easily get it back.

There is false community and true community. There is empowering, supportive community and controlling, exploitive community.

Communities are no different from families. They are in many respects substitute families and all of the abuse patterns you find in dysfunctional families you will find in any kind of social, political, or religious club or grouping.

When human beings gather together in groups, they express the collective worthiness or unworthiness of their members. The higher the sense of worthiness among members, the greater the capacity of the group to love, to support and to serve others.

The Rewards and Costs of Conforming

To some extent all of us compromise when we try to conform to what our families and social institutions expect from us. The word "conform" simply means "with form." Energy is invested in form and expresses therein. To conform means simply to embody.

Now, obviously, form limits what that energy can do and where it can go. Working "with form" means that one will have to accept limits and boundaries. All social behavior in a sense represents some kind of conformity or work within established boundaries and limits.

What society deems appropriate or correct can provide substance and structure to a person who accepts those limits and boundaries, while it can be experienced as imprisoning or confining to someone who does not accept those constraints.

One who conforms willingly gets the direct benefit of belonging to the family, the group, or the society in which s/he lives. One who repudiates convention and rejects the dominant cultural values of his society—unless he belongs to an alternative group—pays the price of isolation and does not get his needs for belonging met.

We all want and need to belong to something greater than ourselves, but (the question for all of is) at what price? Self Betrayal is not a fair price.

On the other hand, we all want to be authentic and true to ourselves, but (the question for all of us is) at what price? If we have to reject others to be ourselves, then we do not meet our emotional needs. We feel cut off, isolated, unsupported, alienated. This also is too high a price.

Therefore the ultimate question is: How can we be ourselves without selling out to the needs and expectations of others or rejecting those needs and expectations in a way that isolates us and cuts us off from the people we love?

If we can see the positive aspect of the word "conformity" we simply realize that there is a natural tension between the needs of the individual and the needs of the group. No matter what we do, where we go, and what group we belong to, this tension will be there. The tension is not bad. It is awakening.

It forces us to move toward finding our highest good.

Finding Our Highest Good

The spiritual law of compassion tells us that our highest good and the highest good of others is one and the same.

What is really good for me cannot in the end be something that is bad for you. And what is really good for you must in the long run be good for me.

In other words, there is a balance to be found between the needs of self and the needs of others, or between the needs of the individual and the needs of the group. Our compassion for self and others helps us find that balance. However, it is ongoing work.

The spiritual student is always asking "What is for my highest good and for the highest good of others?" It is not necessary for him or her to know the answer to the question. It is necessary only that the question be asked over and over again, because in some way the asking of the question points the way toward its answer.

Whereas conformity may result in self-betrayal and non-conformity may result in social rejection, neither extreme is helpful. Most of us need to work with the dichotomous nature of our needs for belonging and individuation to find a healthy synthesis or integration.

Service to Others

The spiritual law of compassion says that all people deserve to have their inalienable needs met. They all deserve life, liberty and the pursuit of happiness. They all deserve to be loved and accepted. They all deserve to have food, clothing, shelter and medical care when they need it.

A compassionate society supports people in achieving physical, emotional and mental health and well being. By doing so, it invests in its people and helps them to self actualize.

Only self-actualized people can give back to the society that nurtured them. Only those who have been fed understand how to feed others.

Service to others cannot be performed by a victim or an unempowered person. Only those who are empowered can empower others. Only those who are loved can love others.

Our goal in serving should not be to do something for others that they should be doing for themselves. That just strips them of their dignity.

It dis-empowers them. It reinforces their belief that they cannot do for themselves. Nor should our goal be to get others to do things the way we like to do them. That is not respectful to their culture or experience.

Our goal should be to empower others to do for themselves and to adapt the resources and methods we share with them to their own unique needs and culture. Then, we will be offering them a real gift, not a golden ball and chain.

If I want to feed you, I can give you the plant or the seed. If I give you the plant and leave you be, you will not learn to plant it and water it and weed it. You might even eat it. But then you will be hungry again. But if I give you the seed and teach you to nurture it, you will understand how it grows and you will be able to plant it again and again. You will learn to feed yourself.

Real compassion doesn't try to feed you. It teaches you to

feed yourself. It doesn't just support you. It teaches you how to support yourself.

Compassion is not about giving people what they do not have. Compassion is about showing people what they already have and teaching them how to use it.

Building an Economy of Love

The Law of Compassion gives birth to the Economy of Love and inclusion.

Most of us try to make a living by sacrifice or trespass. We think we can help others by holding ourselves back. Or we think we can help ourselves by manipulating or controlling others. Neither of these strategies works.

I can't better myself by taking anything away from you. And I can't better you by withholding anything from myself. There are two forms of trespass: cruelty to others and cruelty to self.

There are two forms of greed: taking more than I need and taking less than I need.

The economy of love is not built on sacrifice or on trespass. It is built on free expression and sharing of our gifts. When we do this we generate abundance and the needs of all people can be met.

Humans as a whole generate enough to take care of those who are weak or needy. There is no scarcity of resources. The only scarcity is the lack of willingness of human beings to share and the lack of appropriate distribution and redistribution networks that insure that the resources get to all who need them.

A compassionate society takes care of all of its people. It leaves no one behind. It provides a safety net for those who are not successful in the marketplace as well as for those who become disabled, sick, or too old to be able to engage in healthy competition.

The law of compassion expresses as the desire to care for others. It is all about serving the needs of people and restoring balance, equality and justice in our social institutions.

Generosity (charity) and unselfishness are the positive qualities associated with this spiritual law. Greed and selfishness are the negative qualities that arise when compassion is absent.

Common Needs and Human Affinity

All human beings have similar needs for food, shelter, safety and belonging. We all want to be loved and accepted as we are.

We may come from different races or religions. We might have different values or ideas. But our basic human needs are the same.

We are all born and we all die. Race does not matter when we look death in the eye or experience the death of someone we love. We all have the same pain, the same hopes, the same dreams.

We all belong to the human family. This is our highest level of affinity. It is more important and more transcendent than any other type of affinity: more important than gender, race, religion, economic status, sexual orientation, or political affiliation.

The Affinity Group Process (see my book *Living in the Heart*) was developed to help people join together based on this highest level of affinity. Affinity Groups are small spiritual communities that practice unconditional love and support for their members. Diversity is encouraged. The group does not seek agreement or external results of any kind. That way it can support people unconditionally. Affinity groups offer a safe place where people can feel loved, accepted, blessed, and valued not for what they do, but for who they are in their essence. They are a spiritual oasis that people seek out once per week. For those who do not have a church or temple to attend, they offer a powerful weekly Sabbath experience of joining with other human beings in love and support.

One of the great spiritual crises we are facing today on the planet is that people have lost their families and their sense of belonging to something greater than themselves. They do not have a place to go where they are accepted and loved just as they are. Their families of origin do not offer this and they have not created new families or communities that can provide it.

The truth is it is very hard to love yourself unconditionally without the support of other human beings who are committed to the same goal.

Some people may be able to go it alone on the spiritual path, but most are not able to. They get sucked back into the frantic pace and reactivity of their daily lives. They lose balance and perspective. They forget to love and care for themselves and their families.

The creation of a spiritual family on the local level represents a major turning point on the spiritual path. For with the support of one's Affinity Group one is better able to stay focused on loving self and others.

It is a spiritual law that as we give so do we receive. So the more that we help hold a loving space for others around us the more we create that same loving space for ourselves. And so, thanks to our community, we begin to walk in love, radiating light and warmth to all whom we meet. This is what it means to bear witness. We become the love that we let in.

Twelve Steps and Beyond

One of the great examples of a spiritual community providing service to others is Alcoholics Anonymous (AA) and its various spin off Twelve Step organizations. I doubt very much that the Twelve Steps of AA would have been so successful without the community that embodied the message and created a safe space for people to hear it and internalize it.

There are reasons for AA's success. First, it created a recovery community. It invited people who were suffering to acknowledge their suffering and ask for help. It told them "You are not alone." It broke through the walls of denial, shame and isolation. It told the alcoholic "Here you are acceptable. Here you are a brother or a sister. There isn't any one here who has not gone through the same pain you are going through."

Second, it asked each person to give the gift to someone else. The sponsorship structure insured that the message was passed on from one caring human being to another. And those who took the mantle of teaching and supporting did so with great commitment, even though there were no monetary rewards.

Now in any city in the country you can find an Alcoholics Anonymous meeting to attend. Moreover, the Twelve Step principles have been adopted by many other groups of people with different addictions.

Recovery Groups are a step toward Affinity. In recovery, people share a past of addiction and a mutual desire to be sober or drug free. But once people move beyond their identity as recovering addicts, they still need love, acceptance and support. They need that simply because they are human beings looking for connection with self, with others and with God.

How, Where and from What Do We Recover?

All of us are learning from our mistakes and recovering from our addictions. We may not be addicted to drugs or alcohol. But many of us have developed addictive or compulsive behavior patterns that are harmful to ourselves or others. We have chosen ways to dull or medicate the pain of our lives, perhaps through prescription drugs, or by living our lives in front of a TV screen or video monitor. How many adults spend hours each day visiting pornography sites or chat rooms on the Internet? How many adults are caught in a pattern of infidelity or physical abuse?

It is far easier to disguise our pain and unhappiness than it is to acknowledge it to ourselves and others. Who wants to stand up and proclaim his weakness or his guilt?

Perhaps, more than anything else, what gives us the courage to stand up is seeing other people do it. We see that they are just like us and they are willing to take the risk of trusting their brothers and sisters.

All real service is about building a community of trust and a culture of healing and atonement. It is not about trying to fix others, but about creating a place of safety where people can come to heal.

There is confidentiality in the Affinity group, just as there is in a lawyer's office or a minister's study. We can unburden ourselves and tell the truth without being afraid of being publicly exposed or humiliated.

People in my group are my peers. They are human beings who hurt as I do. They alone can absolve my sins, for they know the pain of my transgression and the relief that comes from its absolution.

I could not come to my group and be this open and vulnerable if my wife or my client were sitting with me. I could not do it if my boss or the Chairman of the Board were there. I need a place where I can express my shame and my remorse without being afraid that someone will judge me or reject me or try to fix me or redeem me.

I am talking about a place where people will listen to me and accept me, not as I might become sometime in the future, but as I am right here and now. I need a place that is deep enough to hold my pain and wide enough to hold all of my transgressions.

When others offer me this kind of safe space, I become willing to take risks. I become willing to look at some of the pain I have caused my loved ones. I become willing to look at how I have tried to control others or how I have allowed others to control me.

I can look at the terrible mistakes I have made, especially the ones I cannot forgive myself for making. I can look at my resentments and my hatreds and my rage against others who have wronged me or humiliated me. I can look at the fact that I do not feel worthy enough to receive the love of my friends and family members, or the love of my Creator.

In our aloneness and separation, we forget a very important fact. We forget that we do not heal alone. Our healing happens on both the personal and collective levels.

My healing inspires and reaches out to you. And your healing gives me the courage to walk through the door when it is opened to me.

This is the basis for the spiritual law of compassion. It is the reason each one of us is led sooner or later to some form of selfless service that enables us to give back to at least one other human being the love and acceptance we have received from another.

7

The Spiritual Law of Perfection

"You weren't given your gift to hide it or hold onto it,
but to cultivate it, bring it forth, and give it
without reservation to all who need it."

The spiritual law of perfection is one of the most misunderstood of all spiritual laws because it has nothing to do with being perfect. Rather, it is about cultivating our talents and abilities and expressing them in the best and most skillful way that we can. It is not about perfection, which is unreachable, but about perfecting, which is an every day affair.

The seventh spiritual law tells us that each human being has a gift to give and he must discover that gift and give it to the world as best he can or he will not achieve his potential. When he is successful in giving his gift, he begins to shine. He lights up and we see him in his unique splendor. If you haven't seen the movie "Shine" (starring Geoffrey Rush) you should do so. It is a cinematic poem expressing all the great themes of the seventh spiritual law.

The Pursuit of Excellence

The seventh spiritual law is not about comparing yourself to others, but about challenging yourself to develop and excel. You may be able to swim only five laps and run only a quarter of a mile when you begin to train. But each day you work out you get stronger. If you are not committed to practice and improvement on a daily basis, you would not be able to run your first 5K race, not to mention your first Triathlon.

No matter what our abilities are, we can develop them. We can be the best we can be. We can fulfill our potential. That is what the law of perfection is all about. Abraham Maslow called it self-actualization.

Healthy competition with others is merely a tool to help us develop ourselves. However, sometimes it works just as well to compete with ourselves. We swim one more lap today than we did yesterday. Or we do a better job recognizing and owning our judgments.

We engage in the perfecting process not because we are broken and need to be fixed, but because we are a work in progress. We are not yet all that we can be. We have unfulfilled or unrealized potential.

Mastery happens only for those who are committed to the

learning process. They learn the basic skills of their craft and practice them constantly. Sometimes they try something and it does not work, but that doesn't discourage them. It just gives them helpful information. For those who are intent on mastery there are no failures; there are only experiences that help them learn what works and what doesn't work.

Self consciousness and the fear of failure are two major obstacles to our achievement of proficiency and eventual mastery. If we are afraid to make a mistake, if we are mortified and beat ourselves mercilessly when we do something stupid, we aren't going to make it through the apprenticeship phase.

Good teachers know this. They don't expect too much of the beginner. They encourage and support him and make light of difficulties. Eventually, the student gains confidence.

When confidence comes in, then the teacher begins to challenge and question the student. He makes the student work. He refuses to let the student settle for a level of skill he can surpass. In the end, the student internalizes the teacher. He becomes his own critic. He refuses to settle for less than he knows is possible. He moves beyond competence and proficiency. He becomes a master of his craft.

This process of perfecting or becoming skilled is the same in any area. There are apprentice electricians and master electricians. There are apprentice violin makers and master violin makers.

Great teachers push their students to improve, but they do not set inappropriately high standards for them or criticize them in a destructive manner. They know when it is time to praise and time to push. That is what makes them great teachers.

They can be infinitely gentle and encouraging. And they can be challenging and confronting if the student has arrogance or false pride.

In the end, the best students surpass their teachers. They learn all that their teachers can teach them and they learn new things on their own.

Teaching and Sharing the Gift

Without a good teacher, a mentor or a role model one respects and admires, one cannot easily learn a skill or a craft. It is not impossible, to be sure. There are always a few self-taught masters around, but they are few and far between. Most students need an interactive process. Most apprentices need feedback on their work to further perfect it.

For the teacher, finding a talented and committed student is a great joy. For mastery means little if the skills learned are not passed on to others.

Yet how many students have the talent to achieve mastery? And, of those, how many are committed to the practice necessary to achieve it?

Luke Skywalker doesn't just show up in Obi Wan's anteroom every day. So you can imagine the teacher's satisfaction when a talented and willing student shows up.

Imagine if you were a great singer but you never got to sing in front of an audience. Something would be missing. To achieve mastery without an opportunity to share, to inspire and to teach means very little.

Each one of us is here not just to realize our potential. We are here to share it with others. We are here to inspire others to find their own gifts and learn to trust them. And we are here to support, encourage and empower others to express their gifts.

The seventh spiritual law is all about giving and receiving. Only those who are given the gift can give it back. One cannot be a student forever.

That is the height of selfishness. The student must teach. He must trust that he is good enough. He must take the risk, however difficult it may be for him, to share who he is and what he can do with others.

Abundance

Without mastery, abundance is impossible to achieve. The apprentice gets things done, but clumsily and ineffectively. As he gains proficiency, things get done more smoothly and efficiently. Finally, when mastery is achieved, things are done beautifully and with great skillfulness. The master makes the most difficult tasks seem easy. It seems they are done not by effort, but by grace.

The notes of the master violinist seem to float on the air, and the bow moves silently and with incredible speed on the strings. A master like Heifetz does not just play the notes. Under his hand the notes come alive. The composer is resurrected from his grave and we encounter the beauty of his work as if for the first time.

Effortlessness and grace are qualities of mastery. They bring an abundance, a harvest not experienced before. When the master

Jesus poured the water, the wineskins filled to overflowing. When he cut the fishes, they began to multiply.

How did he do it? How did Heifetz hit that note? That we may never know. Even the master does not know how he does it.

The truth is, there is a hand behind his hand, a breath behind his breath. If you asked Jesus, he would tell you "I can do nothing lest the Father bids me do it."

Spiritual perfection is completely different from worldly perfection. Spiritual perfection is miraculous. Things get done but you do not know how they get done. You cannot claim authorship, even if it was your hand that pushed the switch.

Miracles are demonstrations of spiritual perfection. We do not know how or why they occur. But we do know that the person through whom the miracle comes surrenders to a consciousness greater than his own. He becomes a vehicle for the expression of the creative love energy of the universe. He is a messenger of God, a divine conduit, one who demonstrates the abundance and grace that are available to us whenever we surrender our limited egoic consciousness to the divine will.

When Jesus gave us the Sermon on the Mount, he spoke of spiritual perfection. He told us that all of our needs could be met through our surrender to God. "Consider the lilies of the field, how they grow. They do not toil, yet see how they prosper."

The seventh spiritual law is about prospering, not by labor, but by grace. The vehicle has been fashioned by committed practice. The instrument has been impeccably tuned. Now it is time for the master to play.

Krishna's Flute

When Krishna plays the flute, the notes resound in all our chakras. We hear and feel the notes, but we don't see all the lifetimes of practice that went into mastering them.

Mastery requires both talent and skill. Years of study, discipline and practice perfect the human vehicle and make it ready for its spiritual work, its divine calling.

Each one of us has a divine calling. We have gifts and talents we need to develop so that we can express the divinity within us. Expressing our calling gives us JOY. It is the work of our hearts. There is no greater experience on earth than that of joyously sharing our gifts.

We know from spiritual law number four that what we really desire and put our energy into comes to pass. If we have a strong desire and an equally strong commitment to our gift, we will gain confidence in it and learn to give it joyfully to others. But that does not happen over night. Most of us do not fulfill our potential early in life. It takes time to understand who we are, to recognize our gift and bring it forth. It requires great dedication and patience. It requires discipline and practice.

If you are not patient and committed, you cannot actualize your potential. Impatience is the great obstacle to right livelihood. A career takes time to evolve. A calling takes even longer.

A Course in Miracles says "Only infinite patience brings immediate results." Try to understand that. If you need immediate results, you are not patient. So be patient and committed and the results will come, perhaps even sooner than you think.

As we achieve mastery we begin to move in the creative flow

of the universal love energy of the universe. We spontaneously attract what we need for our continued progress and growth. We barely have the thought "I need this" when it appears in front of us. Please understand, this is not magic. We are not reciting some secret words or formula. We are simply moving in alignment with ourselves and others.

The more skill we develop in life, the easier it is for us to move in alignment with the Tao.

Once we experience the effortlessness of being "in the flow" of reality as it unfolds, any kind of effort or struggle is unsatisfactory. Why push the river or swim against the tide? It is exhausting and unnecessary.

When we experience the flow, stagnation is no longer acceptable. So we learn to make little adjustments when we feel the energy becoming trapped or blocked. Our attention moves to the obstacle or the blockage and dissolves it, so that the stream of life can move on.

This is not analytical work. It is intuitive. We can feel when we are "off" or when we are "standing in the way" of life. As soon as we feel the tightness or constriction, we move or shift to release it.

This is true physically, emotionally and mentally. We can be "off" in our bodies, in our feelings, and in our thoughts. And we can also adjust and come back into alignment on each level, gradually bringing all levels into alignment with each other and the energy that surrounds us. Correction when seen in this way is neither shameful nor arduous.

When the swimmer feels a pain in the shoulder he eases back and does not pull so hard. Perhaps he takes a break from swimming for a day or two. He lets his body relax and rest.

When the archer misses to the left of the target, he moves his bow slightly to the right. He doesn't even think about this. He does it automatically. His training and sensitivity have prepared him to make correction as the need for it arises.

This is the way we are meant to practice forgiveness. We miss the mark and as soon as we see that, we make an adjustment. If I get angry at you and hurt you, as soon as I see the hurt in your eyes I am pulling my energy back. "I'm sorry," I say, acknowledging the trespass. "That wasn't right. I shouldn't have done that."

And then you can let my trespass go, because I owned it. You see that I did it out of ignorance, impatience, jealousy or some other human weakness.

You don't need me to be perfect. You just need me to be honest and responsible for what I do and say.

Interestingly, there is a direct relationship between our need for perfection and our inability to practice forgiveness. The higher our standards, the more fussy we are, the more we expect from each other, the more difficult it will be for us to forgive ourselves or others.

To protect our self-image, we deny our error. We act like we are right even though we know we aren't. Instead of making correction and moving on, we keep our bow pointed at the same spot and complain that the target is out of place. We blame others. We refuse to take responsibility.

All forms of denial simply make correction more arduous. If I believe that my self worth is somehow on the line when I admit a mistake, I'm not going to admit it very easily. So the block will stay in place. The guilt will fester. The arrow will continue to miss the target.

The truth is that you cannot be happy so long as you need to be right or are afraid to be wrong. Happiness only comes when you can see your error, admit it, and move on.

That is true because happiness and joy are all about "staying in the flow of reality as it unfolds." And any form of denial is a resistance to the flow or an obstacle that must be overcome.

You can't flow with the river if you need to keep stopping to move big boulders out of the way. Can you imagine what would happen to the river if it had to stop every time it encountered a fallen tree or a large rock?

It would not be a river. It would not move on to the sea.

Fortunately, a river cannot pretend not to be a river, so it just goes around all the obstacles in its path and keeps moving.

Humans should learn from the river. Lao Tzu did and so should you and I. When we come to an obstacle, we need to acknowledge it, make a correction and move on.

Forgiveness is not so much about "getting right with God" (although it's fine to think that if you find it helpful). It's more about "staying in the flow."

Judgments, mistakes, misperceptions, trespasses are just temporary interruptions in the flow. A strong river moves easily around them.

When admitting our mistakes becomes "no big deal" and our willingness to correct, apologize or make amends is as automatic as the archer moving his bow an inch or two to the right or the left, then our river will be strong and its journey back to its Source will not be difficult or long.

Forgiveness and Mastery

All masters are not only masters of their craft; they are masters of forgiveness.

At any early age, the pianist learns to forgive his finger when it hits the wrong key and the vocalist learns to forgive her voice when it sings off key. Each learns to make the necessary correction.

Children learn to walk by falling down a lot. If adults make them feel ashamed for falling down, they will not learn to walk. They will become physically and emotionally arrested in that stage of development.

To grow, we must make mistakes and learn from them. That is how we learn to walk, or sing, or play the piano.

We need to be very patient and persistent to learn to do anything in life. And the parents and teachers we have need to be equally patient and encouraging. That is how we learn to trust not just in our talent, but in our capacity to improve and perfect our skills.

We don't realize it, but this kind of constant patience and willing correction of our mistakes is the essence of forgiveness practice.

And please note, I said PRACTICE!

One doesn't learn to be forgiving by doing it once a year, once a month, or even once a week. If you are learning to play the piano your forgiveness practice might be five or six hours per day.

Do we really expect that it would be less if we are learning how to live in harmony with other human beings?

Why Perfectionism Doesn't Work

Perfectionists have the hardest time practicing forgiveness. They take everything personally. They are afraid to make mistakes, afraid of criticism or rejection, afraid to fail. Perfectionists know the quickest way to the cross. They know how to get up on the cross and they know how to put others up there. Their greatest lesson is to learn to be more accepting of the apparent imperfections of life and to be more gentle with themselves and others.

A perfectionist does not achieve mastery, no matter how hard he tries, because he is trying for something that does not exist. Nothing in the world is perfect. Even the greatest master is not perfect.

If the perfectionist wants to be a master, he must ease up on himself and others. He must practice acceptance and forgiveness in each moment. He must become humble and teachable.

All that he can retain from his perfectionist tendencies is his commitment to do the very best that he can. Everything else must go: his pride, his self-consciousness, his harshness with himself and others. He must learn to forgive his mistakes and those of others. He must learn from every error he makes without taking it personally.

It does not matter what your field is. I know guys that have studied Zen who have written books about archery and motorcycle maintenance. They embody the exact same principles.

Mastery is not about what you do. It is about how you do it.

Effort vs Effortlessness

There are two ways to conduct one's life. One is to try to make it happen. The other is to simply allow it to happen. One attempts to manipulate and control. The other simply surrenders and trusts in the process.

The irony of the seventh spiritual law is that unskilled people must rely on manipulation and control because they have cultivated no artistry. On the other hand, skilled people find it easier to surrender and to trust, because they are confident in themselves and their ability.

One must be disciplined and committed to learn a skill. I don't have to tell you how many laps the great swimmer did before he dove into the water in a storm to save a drowning child. He prepared all his life for that one spontaneous act.

A person without his skill and confidence could not have done it. To be sure, a man without skill could have been as brave, but he would not have returned with the child.

We work all our lives to become masters in our field. And our mastery gives us a freedom we could not have without it.

Mastery brings trust in self and trust in the universe. We don't need to "make" anything happen, because our relationship to life is not one of attempting to impose our will on any person or situation. The river teaches us the futility of doing that.

We aren't trying to fix anyone or save anyone. We are not trying to redeem the world. We are not trying to be like Atlas and take responsibility for holding up the world. Overextending ourselves doesn't help others. It just makes it harder for us to be of use.

No, we simply ask "How can I be helpful in this situation?" and the answer comes spontaneously.

The skillful and willing person does not need to deliberate. Her action is clear and concise. She chooses the most helpful option spontaneously and at the best possible time. It seems effortless and it is in a way because it is supported by the universal energy.

When the master acts, she does not act alone. Her action is supported by the universal energies arrayed around her. We call this Grace. And so it is.

Grace

Grace is the alignment of the self with the Self, the human with the Divine. It is an attunement to an energy field of love that originates in the heart and extends outward to all people.

The Miracles of Jesus were acts of Grace. They were actions of the Holy Spirit moving from the heart of Jesus into the hearts of all who asked his help. They were all expressions of love and, as such, they were completely transforming, causing the hearts of others to vibrate at the highest levels of love, if even for an instant.

There are healers like this amongst us today, but that does not mean that you need to go in search of them. For everything they have, you have too. As you attune to the indwelling Spirit of God, you will align yourself with the universal energy and you too will be, in the words of St. Francis, "an instrument" for love and healing in the world.

That is what each one of us is. All of the gifts we have been given and offer to others are gifts of love. They take different forms, but they are made of the same substance.

When the master offers the gift, he knows that God offers it through him. It is not his gift to give, but God's gift. His will and God's will are one and the same or he could not offer the gift.

"Not my will, but Thy will" is both the prayer and the practice of all masters. They do not need personal credit. They do not need name and fame. They need only to be messengers of the Great Spirit. For the messenger is filled up by the Spirit of God. His arms and his legs and his voice vibrate with God's presence and God's love.

There is no greater calling or experience than this. The small self is placed in the service of the Greater Self. And the gift of At-one-ment is given to all.

8

The Spiritual Law of Healing

*"You do not heal alone.
The healing of one aids and abets the healing of all."*

The eighth spiritual law is about healing on all levels. It tells us that all things that are out of balance can come back into balance. Dis-ease can be eased. Error can be corrected. Sin can be forgiven. And guilt can be absolved.

Even if the hiker strays from the path and goes on a great detour, he can find his way back. The alcoholic can become sober and the drug addict can become clean. Those who become lost in codependent relationships and the affairs of the world can return to their connection with Self and with God.

Human beings can fall from grace, but they can also atone.

They can separate from each other and from God, but they can also come back into holy, I-Thou relationships of mutual trust and respect.

Order arises out of chaos. Balance returns after a time of imbalance. It is the nature of the pendulum—swinging back and forth between its poles—to find the center. All healing is about restoring balance and finding our center. It is about reestablishing equilibrium.

The Buddha took the principle of balance as the cornerstone of his teaching. He called it *The Middle Way*. He saw how the attachment to pleasure created a certain type of suffering and how the practice of austerities created a different type of suffering. So he told us not to be attached to pleasure or pain. He told us to find the middle path between these extremes.

No matter how you slice the bacon or roll the dice, extremes tend to lead to imbalance and suffering. Healing then becomes a journey away from extremes to find the center.

When we find the center, we stop our reactive thinking and behavior. We stop bouncing off the walls. We get grounded and grow roots. That is how our spiritual practice deepens. It stops being a seeking after something outside of ourselves, and becomes a looking within our own hearts and minds. Meditation—the core practice of Buddhism—helps us to get rooted in the here and now.

Meditation or other practices of going into the silence are helpful tools for rebalancing and finding the core of our being. We all need to enter the silence on a regular basis to reclaim our center and to keep our lives from spinning out of control.

Yeats wrote "Things fall apart, the center cannot hold." A

strong center is necessary for those of us who lead active lives. The more complex our life is, the more we interact with other people and their ideas, the more crucial it becomes to relax, get quiet and listen within for guidance.

Each of us has spiritual center and when we connect with that center, we hear the truth in a clear way. Regular connection with that center helps us understand the spiritual meaning behind the events and circumstances of our lives. Often that meaning is very different from the one that our friends, family or colleagues see. So if you tend to be easily influenced by the ideas, judgments and convictions of other people, especially those people with whom you live, spending time in silence is an important daily ritual.

Wake up Calls

We are all doing the best we can with the consciousness we have, so let's not be too hard on ourselves or on others. No matter how many good intentions we have, all of us get off track. We take jobs that do not offer us the opportunity to use our talents and abilities. We enter into relationships that are judgmental or hurtful. We make bad decisions that result in injury or illness, financial disaster or shame and humiliation.

It is almost as if life carries a big club and when we begin to move completely out of step with our spiritual purpose, that club whacks us in a place that is certain to get our attention. Of course, no one likes getting whacked. And our first reaction is usually "Why me? What did I do to deserve this?"

Generally, the answer to this question is: It's not so much what you were doing. You might have been getting high, getting fat, being unfaithful to your spouse, or gambling away your life savings. But the whack was not punishing you for doing these things. The whack was not a judgment God was making that "You are a bad boy or girl." No, the whack has a simple message. It stays "Stop wasting time. Stop squandering the talents and resources that have been given to you. Remember your purpose and get on with it. No more excuses."

Is there any one of us that does not get whacked in this way at least once or twice in the course of our lives?

The whack is a wake up call. It is like the Zen master coming behind us when we are meditating and giving us a smack with his stick when he sees us nodding off to sleep.

Even though you don't like being beaten, you aren't going to get mad at the Zen master. You know he isn't hitting you because you are bad, or unworthy, or incompetent or whatever. You know he isn't hitting you out of anger or even judgment.

His action is completely impersonal. He whacks everyone who begins to nod off.

The same is true when some apparently devastating event or circumstance happens in your life. You might get a serious illness or get into a bad car accident. You might come home and find your spouse in bed with the maid or the gardener. You might be fired from your job, go bankrupt, or be convicted of a crime and sent to jail.

At face value, all of these things seem terrible and it is easy to take them personally. It is easy to blame others, to blame yourself, or to blame God. And lots of people do. Lots of people become bitter and don't see the circumstance as an opportunity to shift or to transform their lives.

And then there are people like Mattie Stepanek, the 13 year-old poet who was born with a rare form of muscular dystrophy, and Christopher Reeves, (the actor who played *Superman*) who was thrown off a horse and paralyzed. They step up to the plate and use their tragic circumstance as a rallying call to raise awareness and help others. Their lives become focused and on fire. In spite of their personal pain and struggle, they become emissaries for love and truth. They become an inspiration for thousands, perhaps millions of people.

As many of us know, life is not just about the cards we have been dealt; it is also about how we play them. How we respond to the challenges that face us says a lot about whether or not we lead a meaningful life.

A Wound is a Doorway

Every human being on the planet has a primary wound and healing that wound becomes the most important challenge of her life. At first, she might deny the wound, as well as the anger and the hurt associated with it. But in time she will realize that attempting to disguise or bury the wound does not work. In her attempt to avoid dealing with it, the wound will still be running her life.

Facing our wound takes courage. It takes the willingness to feel our pain and to experience and express our anger. Sometimes we cannot do our healing alone. We need the help of a therapist or of a healing community. Sometimes, we need to see how others have healed to believe that healing is possible for us. Indeed, many people who have experienced healing in their lives have done so with the help of at least one other human being who has overcome similar challenges or obstacles. The decision to heal or to live must come from us. If we have a serious illness or accident and the odds of survival are against us, we have to really want to live to beat those odds. Of course, wanting to live is not a guarantee of success, but it is a prerequisite. If we don't want to live, we probably won't.

The eighth spiritual law is about death and rebirth. Sometimes, we have to make our peace with the fact that our work here is done. We have given as much as we can. We have learned all that we can. We have healed as much as we are willing to heal in this lifetime.

Death is not just a tragedy, although it surely feels like that to loved ones left behind; it is also an act of completion. It is not just a time to mourn the passing of a loved one out of this life, but also a time to celebrate the accomplishments of that person and to express our gratitude for the gifts we have received from him or her.

Sometimes what we think is a wake up call is a call to move on. When the call comes, it is not negotiable. That is why it is important that we live each moment fully and that we do not wait to start offering our gifts to those who need them.

Those who have been close to death and have survived can tell you this emphatically. They might have had little hope or motivation in life until they looked death in the eye but, after that, hope and motivation ceased to be issues for them. They could not delay or procrastinate any more. They knew that death spared them for a reason. They knew that they had something to give that they had not given yet.

A wake up call is a call to live. It might take certain cards out of our hand, but it always replaces them with new cards.

Some wake up calls are a reprieve at death's door, a chance to start over, an opportunity to transform our lives and bring them into alignment with our spiritual purpose. How can you say "No" to such an opportunity?

Discovering Our Purpose

Many people tell me that they have no idea what their life purpose is. They are still trying to decide if they should learn carpentry or study to be a Chiropractor.

I always tell them: do whatever you like. But what you like is your "like purpose" not your life purpose. You can choose your "like purpose," but you can't choose your life purpose. It is not negotiable. You have to do it. You are compelled. It is your gift and you have to give it.

"But I don't know what my gift is," people often tell me.

"That is because you are in denial of your wound," I tell them. "When you deny your wound, you can't find your gift."

"Say that again," they respond. So I say it again, and again and again. You can't find your gift as long as you are in denial of your wound.

Only when you acknowledge the place where you have been wounded, feel the pain of that, and let go of the judgment, the anger or the guilt associated with it, can you begin to heal. And unless you heal, you cannot serve.

All gifts are gifts of love. They are gifts of service. They are a healer's hand reaching back to help a brother or sister who has a pain or a wound that the healer understands, because he or she has been there.

What is your gift? It is faith, hope, courage. It is the willingness to give up falsehood and face the truth. What is your gift? It is your belief in yourself and your brother or sister. It is your belief in God, in the beauty, the purpose and majesty of life.

All gifts are spiritual in nature. And giving them is always some kind of expression of acceptance and love.

Karma, Trespass, Guilt and Forgiveness

Everything that we say or do has a consequence. That doesn't mean that it brings a reward or a punishment. It simply brings a result.

Karma is simply the "result" or consequence of an action.

Jesus told us "As you sow, so shall you reap." What you put out will come back to you (in fact, it never really leaves you, but that is another subject).

Karma does not operate in a linear fashion. It is not an eye for an eye or a tooth for a tooth. The law of Karma is simply the law of healing in operation. It says quite simply that you cannot attack another person without attacking yourself. In the end, you must feel any hurt you have caused.

Attack is a form of projection. We try to give our pain to someone else. We hurt so we want to make someone else hurt.

So we attack and then we feel guilty for the attack. Guilt keeps the attack in our energy field. We think we have given our pain away, but we haven't. It's still there.

Then one day someone comes into our lives or something

happens that triggers our guilt and brings it up for healing. Perhaps we are attacked or hurt by someone else. Perhaps we just see a movie or read a book that shakes us up.

When our guilt rises up and grabs us, the opportunity for healing rises with it. We get a chance to own our trespass and our remorse about what we said or did to another. We get to apologize, make amends or restitution, and ask for forgiveness.

Natural vs. Artificial Guilt

Acknowledging our guilt and owning our pain are the first steps we take into healing and redemption. They take us deeply into the practice of forgiveness, which is the primary way that we bring balance back into our lives.

Because guilt has been a tool used by religion to control people, it is hard for us to see its potential as a powerful tool for healing. To help us see that, we must distinguish between natural guilt and artificial guilt.

Natural guilt is the psychological discomfort (or emotional pain) we experience when we have done something hurtful to ourselves or others. Acknowledging our discomfort and feeling our pain lead to natural remorse and related expressions of sorrow or apology, as well as to heartfelt attempts to repair the damage, make amends or restitution. This is taking appropriate responsibility for our actions.

Artificial Guilt, on the other hand, is discomfort or remorse we feel when we erroneously believe that we have caused someone's pain. We assume a false responsibility. We confess to a crime we did not commit or we let someone give us their guilt.

Now nobody can force us to take on guilt that does not belong to us. We have to be willing to do it.

Why are we willing? Are we carrying some deep shame that we have never looked at? If so, we accept the guilt, even though it does not belong to us. However, this is not a guilt that we can atone for, since we have not trespassed against anyone. In this case, our psychological release cannot come until we look deeper to the underlying shame and heal that.

Artificial guilt is used by our families and social institutions to scare us and control us. There is nothing helpful or pleasant about it. And we must all recognize its toxic nature and refuse to accept blame for events and circumstances we are not responsible for.

We give artificial guilt when we try to blame others or make others inappropriately responsible for our experience. And we receive artificial guilt when we allow others to blame us or inappropriately hold us responsible for their experience.

It is not just the occasional crazy person who confesses to crimes he did not commit. We all do this. And we all accuse others falsely because we are afraid to admit our own guilt.

Spiritual maturity suggests an ability to distinguish between natural and artificial guilt as it arises in our life. Much of our healing on the emotional, mental and spiritual levels is about rejecting the giving or receiving of artificial guilt, healing the shame underneath it, and acknowledging, correcting, and forgiving our natural guilt.

Denial always stands in the way of our taking appropriate responsibility for our thoughts, feeling, words, and actions. So spiritual work is inevitably about breaking down the mechanisms of denial so that we can face the truth about ourselves.

Karmic law insures that our guilt and shame will be acknowledged and brought up for healing. So even if we do nothing to crack our shells of denial, life will eventually do it for us, because sooner or later, appropriate responsibility must be taken.

Most of us are happier when we volunteer to take responsibility than we are when the universe asks us to do so.

Why project your guilt onto others when it just places an unnecessary gap or delay between your sin and its correction? Why involve others in your melodrama if you can discover the root of your pain or your fear and address it?

The wheel of karma is just human beings passing their hurts along and trying to work them out in relationship to each other. It gives us lots of opportunities to look at our stuff and own it, but it is hardly any guarantee that we will.

The karmic wheel isn't fueled by electricity. It is self-sustaining. So it never stops turning.

You don't get off the wheel of karma by stopping it. You get off the wheel of karma by owning your stuff, once and for all.

Spiritual Transformation

We all have amends to be made and stuff to own. We can't keep passing the buck or spinning the bottle.

Our issues go with us and are recreated in every relationship we have. The question is: are we going to own them and deal with them when they come up?

It is not easy to take our focus off of others and put it on ourselves. But that is what spiritual transformation is all about. We stop looking outward and start looking inward. We stop scape-goating and blaming others and begin to look at the fear and the shame that drives our own behavior.

That is sobering stuff. Indeed, isn't that what real sobriety is all about? Real recovery is not just about abstaining from certain substances. That is just the tip of the iceberg. Real recovery is about looking at our pattern of betraying ourselves and blaming others or our pattern of betraying others and blaming ourselves. It is about opening that Pandora's box of self-deceptions and disguises. No one wants to open it, because there are a few hours of mandatory therapy associated with the act.

We don't really want to be in therapy. Yet it's hard to heal or learn to take responsibility without some kind of therapy. We need to go to the heart of the issue, not keep buzzing around it. And the heart of it is not about somebody else. It is about us. It does not matter what others are doing or what others have done to us. That's just the outer buzz before the box is opened.

Open that box of disguises and start digging and at the bottom of the box is a mirror. If you don't want to look into it, you might as well get in the box and close it. It makes a good enough casket anyway.

You are either willing to look at yourself or you aren't. If you are willing to look, you are going to be doing some therapy.

Therapy is simply a modern atonement strategy. It says "I'm willing to face my fears and self deceptions. I'm tired of blaming others for my mistakes and I'm ready to take responsibility for what I am creating in my life."

Saying those words to yourself and/or to another is an atonement moment. It is an invitation to transformation and healing.

It says "I am in pain and I don't want to be in pain anymore." And so the turning point arrives. We get on our knees and ask for help.

The pain that humbles us comes in many forms. It may be substance abuse or addiction. It may be divorce or rejection. It may be losing a job or taking a beating in the stock market. It may be experiencing a a health crisis, an emotional breakdown, or the death of a loved one.

Our lives get dangerously out of balance and we can no longer pretend that everything is okay. Our persona just cannot mask the degree of our pain or dysfunction. Humpty Dumpty is trembling uncontrollably on the wall and we know he is going to crash at any moment.

So we cry out for help. And our cry is heard by all the spiritual beings in the universe. It is the primal, existential cry for truth, for sanity, for an end to suffering. It is the first step in the process of our redemption.

It is a piercing and unmistakable cry. It says "I can't do it any more." The ego agenda has failed and we have admitted it finally. "There must be more than this, Lord. Please help me find it." That is the moment God and his helpers have been waiting for. For without our permission, help cannot be given.

Our healing crisis and our call for help bring the assistance that we need. It may bring us a friend, a therapist, or a sponsor. It may bring us to a therapeutic community where others are going through the same dark night of the soul. Our desire to heal and our willingness to feel our pain inevitably bring us to a safe, loving, place where people are kind to us and know how to hold the space for our healing.

The hands of God are working everywhere in the world. Everyone who has healed from any kind of wound or pain can help someone else heal.

Creating the Houses of Healing for People in Crisis

Since healing is not about denying or avoiding pain, it is not easy. One has to be willing to feel fear, shame, guilt, anger, sadness, resentment, even rage. All the blocks to love's presence must be experienced and dissolved.

One can do that only in a safe and loving place. Staff must be alert, sensitive and compassionate. Great midwives are necessary to guide the caterpillar into his cocoon and to help him emerge as a butterfly.

My friend Elisabeth Kubler Ross created such a safe, compassionate and loving place for dying people. Her work has been monumental in this respect. She has given dignity and respect back to those who are in the midst of one of the most difficult of all transitions.

Today we need hospices not only for those facing physical death, but for those facing emotional and spiritual crisis. One cannot be in the world when one's defense mechanisms are cracking or one's ego is dying. One needs a half-way house, a transitional place.

Similar houses of healing and transition are necessary for young people entering puberty or leaving home, for addicts getting clean or sober, for battered women leaving their husbands, and for prisoners leaving prison.

Schools need designated houses of healing for kids who are in emotional crisis, abusing alcohol or drugs, or who, for other reasons, can't function in traditional classroom settings.

Hospitals need houses of healing for those with cancer or other terminal illnesses.

Houses of healing are necessary to address all four levels on which pain is experienced. We need houses for physical healing, emotionally healing, mental healing and spiritual healing.

When we say "house" of healing, we are not necessarily talking about a place with a roof and four walls. We are talking about a focal area of consciousness and experience.

Each one of us is called to join with others healing from similar wounds and traumas. Our combined talents, interests and abilities are brought to bear on a problem or issue that we feel passionate about. Usually, it is connected to the place where we have been most deeply wounded. Because we need to heal in this place, we can help create a healing community for others with similar wounds. Our gift and our authentic spiritual calling usually arises out of the discovery of our own House of Healing.

The Great Work of our Time

The early Christian communities were healing houses, affinity spaces, places of acceptance and forgiveness. They were the social mechanisms of redemption. Our challenge is to recreate these small loving communities devoted to supporting people unconditionally.

This is the great work of our time. There are no bystanders or sideliners in this work. There are only heartfelt participants.

This is not a work that can be done half-heartedly or with an ego-agenda. It must be done with conviction and with an open heart.

This is not a work that can be done by government agencies or by other large, bureaucratic institutions. It can be done only by small dedicated groups of people. This is not a work that seeks to make a profit for any person or company. It is service and healing work offered on a not-for-profit basis.

We don't realize it, but atonement is a collective healing process. Most of us do not heal alone. We heal with each other.

The great mission of Jesus Christ was to bring us the message of our shared healing. Whenever one person wakes up, the light on earth increases exponentially. It is like adding a zero to any number. One becomes ten and ten becomes a hundred.

When one person masters all ten spiritual laws, his light expands tenfold, perhaps even a hundredfold. People who are hungry for the teaching find their way to his doorstep.

From one committed teacher, another ten teachers emerge. Thus, the spiritual community touched by the first teacher expands to hundreds, perhaps even thousands.

In his time, Jesus spoke to thousands. Since then his teaching has reached billions. Of those, one was a St. Francis. One was a Ghandi. One was a Mother Theresa. And each of them had their own ministries bringing others to truth, to freedom and into the lap of unconditional love and compassion.

You do not have to compare yourself to other teachers to understand your important place in the collective atonement process. Every teacher has students who are waiting for him or her to leave the desert and begin teaching.

Your students are waiting. That is not an invitation to rush or skip steps. Your healing must take as long as you require. But it is a message that time is of the essence. Your awakening and the healing that it brings to others is important. It is valuable. Indeed, it is sacred. You need to trust it.

No one thinks she is worthy to teach or heal until God blesses her and sends her forth. But then she knows in her heart and never looks back.

We do not teach or heal for personal glorification, but for the glorification of God. Without God's love and guidance, we would not be up to the task. But because of it, we can do all that is given to us to do.

You and I have powerful companions. We are asked to witness and to serve. But we are not asked to do it alone.

The help that we need will be given to us. In this, we must learn to trust. And the more we trust, the more it shall come to pass.

9

The Spiritual Law of Individuation

"You must become who you are and leave the rest behind."

The spiritual law of individuation tells us that each one of us is destined to become who we really are. Our destiny is to manifest our essence fully and completely.

When we have the courage to be ourselves under any circumstances, we have true freedom. We no longer have to live our lives in someone else's shadow or to overshadow others. We no longer need to give our power away or claim a false power to make decisions for others.

Interestingly, as soon as we empower ourselves fully, we simultaneously empower others. We know that we cannot be free to be ourselves unless we also give others freedom to be themselves.

All the masks and chains come off when we individuate. All power plays are off limits. Specialness dissolves and equality with other human beings is the rule and the measure of our lives.

People who do not complete the personal and social healing piece that is called for by the eighth spiritual law will inevitably make a mockery of the principle of individuation. They will use it to justify their own empowerment without returning the favor to others. They will entice others to help them carry out their selfish agendas with promises of reciprocity that are never fulfilled.

So let us be clear. Individuation does not mean selfishness. It is not just about personal power. It is about universal power—the power of God—vested within a person. That is where inner authority comes from. It is the power of the divine essence inside each one of us.

Those who individuate become the footsoldiers of the divine, or as St. Francis would say, they become "instruments" of God's will. They witness to the truth in their own unique way and often are called to uphold it in the face of injustice.

The words and actions of such a person must be beyond reproach. What they say and do must benefit self and others equally. Such a person has no enemies. If he does, then he is not individuated. An individuated person loves his neighbor as himself, even if he disagrees with him. He does not attack others. He may challenge their words or their actions, but he does not put them down, question their worthiness, or seek to shame or humiliate them. His love extends equally to those with whom he disagrees as it does to those with whom he agrees. His love is not based on agreement. It is based on acceptance and respect.

When you accept the God in yourself, you accept the God in others too. You fulfill the spiritual law of equality and demonstrate it in all that you say and do.

A teacher who claims authority without practicing equality is not individuated. He's on a power trip. This is a simple and clear yardstick that all spiritual students can use to distinguish the true spiritual teachers from the false ones.

A Jewel in the Heavenly Crown

As we re-enter unity consciousness, we do so with the full force of our uniqueness intact. Each of us is a one-of–a-kind jewel reflecting the light of our creator.

A lot of people think we must surrender our individuality to experience God. But that is not the case.

We surrender our egos, but not our uniqueness. We surrender all that separates us from God and from each other. But we do not surrender our essence or its unique, authentic expression.

In other words, when you become individuated, you don't stop being "weird." If anything you become more "weird."

That is because all that is false falls away. All artificial, externally imposed customs and conventions dissolve. The fire of the emerging divinity burns all this away, leaving only what is genuine.

In other words, the self-realized person becomes who She really is with no apology. She does not need to please nor does she need to offend. She does not need your approval or your attention. She is content to be herself in all situations and circumstances.

This is an unedited and unrepressed person. She is on fire with the truth and she burns bright.

You might love her or hate her, but you can't pretend not to see her or hear what she has to say. Where others waver and give in, she stands firm. Even if she fears death, she does not let that fear hold her back from speaking the truth in each moment. Her commitment to Truth is certain and irrevocable.

The Practice of Detachment

Detachment is one of the core teachings of the Buddha and one of the essential concepts and practices of the Ninth Spiritual Law. Indeed, you might say, it is the bridge from the Ninth Law to the Tenth Law, from Individuation to Enlightenment.

The first thing that we must understand is that we cannot detach from anything until we are ready. As long as our desires need to be fulfilled, as long as we have requirements or expectations, we will not be able to detach.

The Third Chinese Patriarch of Chan Buddhism wrote in his verses on the Faith Mind: *"The Way is not difficult for those who have no preferences."*

It is true, but of course most of us have preferences. We want things to be a certain way.

However, at a certain point in our spiritual development, we see the childishness of our desires and preferences. The little kid inside wants his cookie and he isn't going to be happy until he gets it. So we give it to him from time to time, but we tell him that one of these days that cookie might not be available. "While you eat this cookie," we tell him, "prepare for that day."

You know the expression "you can't have your cake and eat it too?" It's kind of like that. Once you eat it, you don't have it.

Of course, this isn't a very popular concept these days. We new age babyboomers are not happy just having our cake. We definitely want to eat it too. We want the purple aura over our heads and the Mercedes in the driveway.

We don't want to hear that a time of "not having it" is coming for all of us. We don't want to hear that the Mercedes has got to go, even though we know we aren't going to be able to take it up to heaven with us.

Jesus told us "Do not store up your treasures on earth where moths and rust will eat them." He was telling us the same thing.

The Buddhists are quite serious about the practice of detachment. In some Buddhist traditions the monks go to the crematory and sit next to the skulls to understand the impermanence of life.

Nothing that is here lasts forever. In the end of this journey, the body will have to be relinquished. The great Buddhist teachers would tell you "Even while you enjoy this body and care for it, remember it too will go."

That's just a little heavier version of the cookie mantra.

The spiritual practice of detachment goes hand in hand with understanding the impermanence of our earthly experience. Nothing of this world lasts forever. Everything must eventually be relinquished.

The truly authentic, self-realized individual lives as Jesus asked us to live. She lives in the world, but she is not of the world.

She lives in a body, but she knows on a moment to moment basis that one day that body will be surrendered.

Living in the Present

As we move out of duality consciousness back into unity consciousness, we begin to live more and more in the present moment. Indeed, our sense of the present expands to include the past and the future.

Increasingly, we see that everything is contained in the expanded present. Everything that has ever been and everything that could ever be is fully present right now. That is the consciousness of the spiritual master.

What does it mean to live in the present?

It means "no regrets about the past." It means guilt has been acknowledged and released. There has been forgiveness of self and others. And forgiveness is practiced moment to moment as a way of life.

It means "no expectations of the future." One accepts that the future is mysterious and unknowable, yet divinely guided. One surrenders expectations, brings one's attention to what is happening now, and trusts the future to unfold according to the divine will.

The willingness to Trust replaces the need to control.

Moving Back into Oneness

The individuated person has healed the split within her own consciousness between shadow and persona, between spiritual adult and wounded child.

With no more division within consciousness, there can be no more projection. All forms of denial, resistance and refusal to take responsibility are dissolved and one neither has nor makes any more enemies in the world.

The so called "problems" of life are experienced as waves rising and falling on the ocean of consciousness. One is not attached to the highs or the lows but goes willingly wherever life dictates.

The self-realized human being lives spontaneously in the flow of reality as it unfolds and any snags, obstacles or resistances are quickly surrendered by breathing and letting go.

She does not take herself or others too seriously. She is playful and can laugh easily at human foibles and the absurdity of life.

For the master, there is no longer any question about whether human beings are good or evil, worthy or not worthy. Only goodness and worthiness are perceived. When confronted by those who are fearful and in pain, the only response possible is love and compassion.

The master cannot criticize. She can only bless. She cannot complain for there is nothing to complain about.

Living in Unity consciousness means living in the awareness that all is good and everyone is acceptable just as he or she is.

There is no desire to fix, save, change, edit or redeem anyone. The master loves and accepts. She does not proselytize or preach. For her, there are no problems, no worries, no needs or insufficiencies. There is always enough right here and now.

The Marriage of the Human and the Divine

In a sense there is nothing remarkable about the Master. Even Master Jesus was just a human being among human beings. He was not special and indeed any specialness claimed by him would have prevented him from being a messenger of God.

We want to make our holy men and women special. We want to endow them with superhuman qualities. We want to single them out and raise them up onto a pedestal, just like we do with movie stars. But real masters don't let us do that, because it is a hindrance in their work and in our spiritual development.

False teachers like to be raised up on a pedestal because they are attached to name and fame and riches. They do not practice the principle of equality in their lives. They are always talking about the good guys and the bad guys. They cannot help doing that because they are still living in duality consciousness.

But true masters turn down the spotlight. They do not need name, fame or money. They do not need to be perceived as special. They are content to be ordinary human beings.

This is deeply troubling to us. The idea that Jesus might be a bit of a schlep pushes our buttons. He has to be like Charlton Heston playing Moses. We have to see the Red Sea parting with dazzling special effects to be satisfied. We want heroes, not teachers; saviors not equal brothers and sisters.

But how can someone who teaches the Spiritual Law of Equality as a cornerstone of his teaching be anything else than an equal brother or sister? If he needed to be special, there would be hypocrisy in his teaching, a troubling gap between his words and actions.

Jesus called the Pharisees hypocrites for that reason. They were on the take. They were protecting their power and position. They used the law to their own ends; they didn't care about its true meaning, nor did they feel called to model it.

The man who overturned the tables of the moneylenders and knocked over the priestly pedestals wasn't about to mount the stage and call himself "the only son of God." That would have been the utmost blasphemy, not just for a Jewish teacher, but for any teacher of radical equality.

So we have a lot to learn when it comes to understanding who the real masters are. Remember, Charlton Heston was not Moses. He just played Moses. Actually, he is the president of the NRA and I don't think Moses is on the Board.

If you want to understand real mastery, let's look to the example of a different actor: the one who played Superman. When his wake up call came, he went from a Hollywood pedestal to a wheel chair. He couldn't play Superman any more. But that is when he stepped into the fullness of his life. That was when he found his true calling and began to carry it out impeccably.

We don't like the idea of a wheelchair master, but that's the reality of life. One of our greatest presidents was a wheelchair president.

If you met Christ today, he might appear totally ordinary: no flowing hair and no long robe. He might be a Hispanic laborer picking grapes or a black orderly in a hospital gown.

It isn't easy for us to give up our pictures, even though we know they are absurd. Who is the real superman? It's not the guy Christopher Reeves played in the movie. It's the guy in the wheelchair who is serving God, bringing the message of hope and love to those who are crying out for it.

Simplifying Life

At a certain point on our spiritual path we begin to realize that it is time to simplify our lives. We have so much stuff, so much paperwork, so many things to do and places to go. We spend all our time buzzing around and we don't have anything much to show for it. We are tired of life as a rat race. So we begin to pare down. When the dog dies, we don't run out and get another one. When children move out, we don't give them a round-trip ticket. When someone admires one of our plants or our couch, we say "Please, take it. I'd love to give it to you."

In India, it is traditionally appropriate for a householder to become a monk and leave home when his children are grown. The first part of life is for acquiring possessions and taking care of children and family. The second part of life is for gaining spiritual understanding. So it is natural to let go of the possessions and all the busy routines necessary to maintain them. You don't have to justify your decision or write long letters to your friends and family. You just put a few things in a sack, grab your loin cloth, and hit the trail.

There comes a time when we all have to cut ourselves loose.

We don't necessarily need to cancel all of the insurance policies and give all our money to charity. However, we must begin to lay our burden down in some substantial way.

It's hard to devote yourself to spiritual practice when you are working 9 to 5 every day and when your life is one long subway ride between high rises. That's not to say that you can't be in the world and not of the world. Surely, it is possible.

But the truth of the matter is that unless you have detached from the affairs of the world, it very difficult to be in the world without getting lost in the reactive melodrama. Ninety-nine percent of the people who try fail.

So the work of detachment and simplification must begin if you are a serious spiritual student. Priorities must shift.

The Wandering Mystic

The number nine is the number of the wandering mystic. Lao Tzu was such a man. He lived in the forest and from time to time would appear in the villages and give counsel to the leaders. Then he would disappear again on the path up the mountain or along the river. He was a poet and a mystic. He was not seeking anything in the world.

If you met him on the mountain trail, you would think "'That's a bit of a ragged man." You would completely overlook him, unless you happened to look into his eyes. And you better hope you didn't do that or you would be lost forever.

In those eyes you could see and feel a vast emptiness that drew everyone and everything into itself.

He was like the guy Moses met on his way up to Mt. Sinai. Moses mistook him for a burning bush, but he knew he was in the presence of God. Imagine, he could have just walked passed him and avoided his eyes, but he could not do so. You wouldn't be able to either.

When Jesus came to the small fishing village, he called to Simon and his friends "leave your nets." And they too made the same mistake of looking into the master's eyes. Once they did, it was all over.

They left their jobs and their families. They became disciples. They became the ones who would midwife the work and create the first Affinity Communities.

Do not think that you are not asked to do the same. If you hear the call, you must follow it. You cannot pretend that you are too busy or preoccupied to hear it.

The Call of the Heart

The call is a simple one. It says to us "Wake up to your true Self. Come and join with others in creating a safe, loving place for awakening. Help us hold the space for ourselves and extend it to others."

It is not glamorous work. We still have to chop wood and carry water. We still have to take care of ourselves and other people. But now we are learning to do this without attachment.

The more we surrender, the better we hold the space. Sometimes our buttons get pushed, and we have to ask others to hold the space of love and compassion for us. Sometimes their buttons get pushed and we are asked to hold the space for them.

We are all human. We are all divine.

Sometimes our work is in the fields and in the gutters. Sometimes it is in the meadows and on the mountaintops.

We have to be present wherever we are and go wherever we are needed. That is what the call is all about. The more flexible we are, the easier it is to hear the call and follow it.

We all need the support of our spiritual families and communities, but we are also asked to carry the torch by ourselves. We are asked to tread where only angels have tread before us, carrying the message of love, equality, and peace.

Of course, we are tested and challenged along the way. Our fears still rise up and we learn to hold them gently so that we can continue on the path.

Most importantly, we learn that wherever we go, God goes with us and we learn to rely less on ourselves and more on Him.

Often, we have no idea what to say, yet if we trust, the words will come. The message will be given through us.

Often, we have no idea what to do, but if we breathe and trust as we move forward, a door will open for us.

The great masters move effortlessly from place to place, but they never know where they will be going tomorrow. They simply show up with the willingness to put one foot in front of the other and they are guided which way to go.

The law of change and uncertainty does not immobilize them. They understand it and have learned to work with it.

They do not need to know what they will do, what they will say, or where they will go in advance. They have surrendered and continue to surrender the need to know or to control. They have learned to rest in their divine ignorance and trust the universe in its inherent wisdom and grace.

The Spiritual Law of Enlightenment

*"Be certain: from whither you have come,
to that place you will return."*

It is hard to talk about the Law of Enlightenment or Transcendence because words are inadequate. Suffice it to say, it is the last step of the spiritual journey. In this final step, we return to God: the Source from whence we came.

While we may understand the number 1, or 01 to be more accurate, as the creation (of ADAM), the number 10, represents the reception of the awakened ADAM or any other monad or singular presence, back into the Allness of God. It is a movement from differentiation back into oneness. That is why it is so hard to describe, because that which is separate from the whole, even by a hair, disappears when it is absorbed back into the whole.

In this final step on the Journey, Adam rejoins God and ceases to be Adam. Of course, this is the moment we all dread until we have moved into the level of spiritual mastery denoted by the number 9. At that point, we are already significantly detached from the world of form and the final surrender to the Creator does not scare us anymore.

The final step is not taken by us. When we are ready we are simply absorbed back into divine love and intelligence. By then, we have no further need to be Paul, or Ralph, or Jesus.

That is what happened to Jesus and Buddha and all the enlightened ones.

Atman, the individual soul, returns to Brahman, the Creator. The ten thousand things return to Tao, or Essence, or Source.

The manifest journey is over and individual At-One-Ment is complete. Yet those who have returned to God continue to light the way for those who have not completed the journey. Their footsteps are illumined in the energy fields or fields of consciousness we pass through as we move forward on our own journeys. When we come to one of those places that has particular relevance or importance to us, we tune into the consciousness of the teacher or teachers who were there before us. Although they are not in form, we are able to establish a direct energetic connection to their essence. And that connection guides and supports us until we come to the next critical place on our journey.

Some of us resonate with the same teacher and teaching throughout our journey. Others of us move on to different teachers as we grow in consciousness. Yet, it is not unusual to be attuned to several teachers and teachings at the same time.

What we call angels or other spiritual beings are simply resonating fields of consciousness that have been pulled back to their spiritual center or place of origin and have left their energetic memory or calling card for us to find.

When enlightenment or transcendence comes, the individual is no longer attached to his physical body. He can lay it down at any time. This is the state Jesus reached when he prepared for his crucifixion. It is a state of freedom that is rarely attained on the planet. In this state, there is no fear of death, for one has already experienced that which was prior to birth and will be after death.

After physical death, embodiment continues in mental/emotional sheaths or energy bodies. As one grows in consciousness, one has other death/rebirth experiences as one continues to transition into progressively refined energy bodies and to share in the energy fields of others on that level. Each soul seeks its appropriate level based on its capacity to understand and to love. All this is determined by the resonance or vibration of consciousness itself.

That is why death per say does not result in enlightenment. However, it may lead to a psychological letting go and detachment that prepares one for a higher vibration of non-physical experience.

All major transitions in life are doorways to greater love and wisdom. That is why Jesus told us "You have to die and be reborn to enter the kingdom of heaven." Every time something untrue dies in us, the truth is energized and we are given the opportunity to vibrate with it at a higher level of consciousness.

The highest levels of consciousness are simply those in which there is very little if any untruth, deception or illusion.

In this life and in all other lives—physical or non-physical— we are constantly surrendering a lesser experience for a greater one. The more consciousness expands, the more refined a body or energy field it requires.

Returning Home

The tenth spiritual law states that all of us will eventually return to our Source.

The fact that Jesus, or Buddha, or Lao Tzu, or Rumi or the Baal Shem Tov could achieve enlightenment while in the body is a promise to all of us that we too can wake up fully.

As I have pointed out in my book *Enlightenment for Everyone,* the light is within each one of us. We do a good job of hiding it or covering it up, but when we look deeply enough into any one's eyes, we can see the light of truth reflected there.

Enlightenment is simply awakening to the truth that is already there in each one of us. It is becoming fully who we already are. The more we trust and nurture the spiritual spark within the more it grows into a steady flame until we are virtually on fire with the truth. As each one of us lights up, we radiate divine love and wisdom to all we meet.

That is how the vibration of the collective human consciousness is lifted up. The more people awaken to the truth within and begin to trust it, the more earth vibrates in resonance with that truth and the more the planet becomes a place of healing and support for all its inhabitants. The houses of healing spring up everywhere and the love of Christ, the compassion of the Buddha, the wisdom of Lao Tzu, and the gifts of all the great masters become embodied through us.

In Judaism, the Shechinah—the Spirit of God in exile in the world—cannot return to its Source until all souls are redeemed. As long as one soul continues to live in darkness, in pain, or ignorance, the Messiah cannot come and the final (collective) redemption cannot occur.

The coming of the Christ or Messiah is not a moment of judgment of the good vs. the evil, or the believers vs. the non-believers, as fundamentalist Christians would have it. Rather, it is a celebration of an at-one-ment that will have already occurred in the collective consciousness of human beings. To talk about this event is absurd, because when it happens, none of us will be here to have the discussion.

The metaphor of the second coming does not point to Jesus coming back to earth in another body, but to the human family finally attaining Christ Consciousness. It points to the final absorption of human, dualistic consciousness into unity or divine consciousness.

When earth comes to heaven, heaven will come to earth. Will that be a new Garden of Eden, an earthly paradise, a time of peace and unconditional love for all human beings on the planet? Or will it mean that the planet itself dissolves and disappears?

Indeed, does it matter at all?

Every Buddhist monk or nun takes a vow not to enter Nirvana (the final merging with God) until all sentient beings have been saved. Indeed, they need not take that vow, for it is the law of heaven itself. Until all are lifted up, the Created cannot fully return to its Creator.

Even a single being in pain holds the collective At-one-ment back. And as long as one person feels unloved, or unworthy, or afraid, his cry for help will be heard throughout all the universes. And so it should be.

God does not abandon us. Christ does not abandon us. Buddha does not abandon us.

All who ascend to the heavenly realms as well as their disciples and helpers here on earth and in the non-physical realms are available to guide us and to help us heal. We have only to ask their help, and someone will come who is uniquely qualified to answer our call.

All spiritual beings distribute energy to those in need at their vibratory level. There is a chain of consciousness and a chain of help available to all of us at all times.

Tuning into the help and the guidance that is there for us is the most important thing that we can do. We do this through prayer, meditation, singing, dancing, chanting, walking in the forest or by the sea. We do this by opening our hearts to love and our minds to truth.

We are all on the journey back to God. That is the good news. And there is more good news than that. We do not have to rush. We do not need to panic. All we have to do is take a deep breath and be present right here and right now.

For the enlightened ones, this moment is perfect just the way it is. There are no problems, no mistakes, no inadequacies or insufficiencies.

Now is timeless and eternal. Here is everywhere. Thus there

is nowhere else to go and no other time or place to be.

Questions about anything other than that which is right now or right here begin to seem absurd and irrelevant. In the end they merely drop away.

Certainty replaces uncertainty,
truth replaces untruth,
being replaces becoming,

As love grows and extends to all,
the fear of death, annihilation, or non-existence
drops away

Even whether one lives or dies
has no great significance,
as one transcends the limits of physical life.

The more we merge
with the Eternal Self
that is not born and cannot die,
the more we relinquish
all that separates us from each other
or from God.

This was our state at the beginning
of our incarnational journey
and it is our state at the end of it.

Everything else is a dream
fueled by the belief in a separate self
and the fear and guilt associated with that belief.

Here, visible dies into the invisible,
seen into the unseen,
presence into omnipresence.

Manifest returns to unmanifest,
form to the formless,
the particular to the universal
the part to the whole,
which is complete and indivisible.

Here, the only time is now,
which is eternal,
and the only place is here,
which is infinite.

Here, that which seems stationary
is actually moving
at the speed of light,
and that which seems to be moving
is dying into that stillness,
at the center
of the turning wheel.

Here sound dies into soundlessness
like the silence in the eye
of a hurricane.

Here end merges into beginning,
periphery into center,
something into nothing.

That which is ubiquitous (existing everywhere)
cannot be seen.
It is the like the background
against which all others things read out.

That which is eternal (always present)
cannot be discerned.
Since it never ceases to be,
no one sees it appear or disappear.

God cannot be expressed in words.
Yet when we try we say:
It is smaller than the smallest particle
and larger than all the manifest universes.

Both its smallness and its greatness are infinite.
Even the longest rope cannot encompass it.
Even the sharpest knife cannot dissect it.

That is why the Taoist just call it
The Tao.

It is the highest teaching on the planet.

Beyond this, there are no words or concepts,
only indescribable experiences.

Paul Ferrini is the author of over 30 books on love, healing and forgiveness. His unique blend of radical Christianity and other wisdom traditions goes beyond self-help and recovery into the heart of healing. His conferences, retreats, and *Affinity Group Process* have helped thousands of people deepen their practice of forgiveness and open their hearts to the divine presence in themselves and others.

For more information on Paul's work, visit the web-site at *www.paulferrini.com,* email: info@heartwayspress.com or write to **Heartways Press, 9 Phillips Steet, Greenfield, MA 01301.**

New Releases from Heartways Press

Paul Ferrini's *Course in Spiritual Mastery*

Part One: The Laws of Love
A Guide to Living in Harmony
with Universal Spiritual Truth
144 pages $12.95
ISBN # 1-879159-60-0

Part Two: The Power of Love
10 Spiritual Practices that Can Transform
Your Life
168 pages $12.95
ISBN # 1-879159-61-9

Part Three: The Presence of Love
God's Answer to Humanity's Call for Help
160 pages $12.95
ISBN # 1-879159-62-7

Paul's In-depth Presentation of the Laws of Love on 9 CDs

THE LAWS OF LOVE
Part One (5 CDs) ISBN # 1-879159-58-9 $49.00
Part Two (4 CDs) ISBN # 1-879159-59-7 $39.00

Audio Workshops on CD

Seeds of Transformation:
5 cd set includes: Healing Without Fixing, The Wound and the Gift, Opening to the Divine Love Energy, The Laws of Love, The Path to Mastery.
5 CDs   ISBN 1-879159-63-5 $48.00

Two Talks on Spiritual Mastery
by Paul Ferrini
We are the Bringers of Love   CD 1
Surrendering to What Is   CD 2
2 CDs   ISBN 1-879159-65-1 $24.00

Love is That Certainty
ISBN 1-879159-52-X $16.95

Atonement: The Awakening of Planet Earth and its Inhabitants
ISBN 1-879159-53-8 $16.95

From Darkness to Light:
The Soul's Journey of Redemption
ISBN 1-879159-54-6 $16.95

Relationship Books

Dancing with the Beloved: Opening our Hearts to the Lessons of Love
ISBN 1-879159-47-3
160 pages paperback $12.95

Living in the Heart:
The Affinity Process and the Path of
Unconditional Love and Acceptance
128 pages paperback ISBN 1-879159-36-8
$10.95

Creating a Spiritual Relationship
128 pages paperback
ISBN 1-879159-39-2 $10.95

The Twelve Steps of Forgiveness
120 pages paperback ISBN 1-879159-10-4
$10.95

The Ecstatic Moment:
A Practical Manual for Opening Your Heart
and Staying in It.
128 pages   paperback   ISBN 1-879159-18-X
$10.95

Christy Mind Books

Part 1   Part 2   Part 3   Part 4

Love Without Conditions ISBN 1-879159-15-5 $12.00
The Silence of the Heart ISBN 1-879159-16-3 $14.95
Miracle of Love ISBN 1-879159-23-6 $12.95
Return to the Garden ISBN 1-879159-35-x $12.95

The Living Christ ISBN 1-879159-49-X paperback $14.95
I am the Door hardcover ISBN 1-879159-41-4 $21.95
The Way of Peace hardcover ISBN 1-879159-42-2 $19.95
Reflections of the Christ Mind hardcover $19.95

Wisdom Books and Audio

Everyday Wisdom
A Spiritual Book of Days
224 pages paperback $13.95
ISBN 1-879159-51-1

Wisdom Cards: Spiritual Guidance
for Every Day of our Lives
ISBN 1-879159-50-3 $10.95
*Each full color card features a beautiful
painting evoking an archetypal theme*

Forbidden Fruit: Unraveling the Mysteries
of Sin, Guilt and Atonement
ISBN 1-879159-48-1
160 pages paperback $12.95

Enlightenment for Everyone
with an Introduction by Iyanla Vanzant
ISBN 1-879159-45-7
160 pages hardcover $16.00

The Great Way of All Beings:
Renderings of Lao Tzu
ISBN 1-879159-46-5
320 pages hardcover $23.00

Grace Unfolding: The Art
of Living A Surrendered Life
96 pages   paperback   ISBN 1-879159-37-6 $9.95

Illuminations on the Road to Nowhere
160 pages   paperback
ISBN 1-879159-44-9 $12.95

Audio Books

The Economy of Love Readings from *Silence of the Heart,
The Ecstatic Moment, Grace Unfolding* and other books.
ISBN 1-879159-56-2 $16.95

Relationship as a Spiritual Path Readings from *Creating a
Spiritual Relationship, Dancing with the Beloved, Miracle of Love* and other
books. ISBN 1-879159-55-4 $16.95

The Hands of God Readings from *Illuminations, Enlightenment
for Everyone, Forbidden Fruit, The Great Way of All Beings* and other
books. ISBN 1-879159-57-0 $16.95

Love Without Conditions Read by the author, 3 CDs.
3.25 hours ISBN 1-879159-64-3 $36.00
Also available on cassette tape for $19.95

Order any of these products on our website:
www.paulferrini.com

or call toll free in the US: 1-888-HARTWAY

The website has many excerpts from
Paul Ferrini's books, as well as information
on his workshops and retreats.

Be sure to request Paul's free email newsletter,
his inspirational weekly wisdom message,
and a free catalog of his books
and audio products.

Heartways Press
9 Phillips Street
Greenfield, MA 01301
413-774-9474   Fax: 413-774-9475
www.heartwayspress.com
email: info@heartwayspress.com..